CW00739626

BRISTOL CHANNEL AND SEVERN PILOT

Other cruising guides and pilots published by Stanford Maritime

Baltic Southwest Pilot
by Mark Brackenbury

Brittany and Channel Islands
Cruising Guide
by David Jefferson

Cruising French Waterways
by Hugh McKnight

Frisian Pilot: Den Helder to
the Kiel Canal
by Mark Brackenbury

Norwegian Cruising Guide
by Mark Brackenbury

Scottish West Coast Pilot:
Troon to Ullapool, and the
Inner Hebrides
by Mark Brackenbury

BRISTOL CHANNEL AND SEVERN PILOT

Peter Cumberlidge

Sketch Charts compiled and drawn by Jane Sandland

STANFORD MARITIME LIMITED · LONDON

Stanford Maritime Limited
Member Company of the George Philip Group
27A Floral Street London WC2E 9DP
British Library Cataloguing in Publication Data
Cumberlidge, Peter
    Bristol Channel and Severn pilot.
    1. Yachts and yachting—Bristol
    Channel   2. Navigation Bristol Channel
    I. Title
    623.89′223′37   GV817.G7

ISBN 0-540-07422-5

Typeset by Tameside Filmsetting Limited,
Ashton-under-Lyne, Lancashire
Printed in Great Britain by BAS Printers Limited,
Over Wallop. Hampshire

Contents

Acknowledgements

This pilot book owes much to the assistance and co-operation received from a great many yachtsmen, harbour masters, and others connected with cruising in the Bristol Channel. I am especially grateful to the following people for kindly letting me tap their local knowledge of these waters, and for helping to double-check the accuracy of the detailed sailing directions.

Dennis Davies, Roger Fry, Keith Hadley, George Hart, David Hawell-Jones, Jim Hewitt, Brian James, Charles James the Managing Director of Swansea Yacht Haven, Govan Johns the Manager of Camper & Nicholson's Marina at Milford Haven, Morton Jones, Jan Miles, Dave Pezzack, Bob Pickstock, Tony Preedy, Derek Scott the Coxswain of the Mumbles Lifeboat, Mr S. Snelling, Tom Tummuscheit, Barry Webb, Colin Wilkins, G. E. Woollard the Chairman of the Amalgamated Gloucester Pilots Committee, and Bill Young.

The sketch charts in this book have been drawn by Jane Sandland. Some are based on charts published in the 7th Edition of the *Bristol Channel Yachting Conference Handbook*. For many years this excellent, locally-published guide has provided the only source of pilotage information for the smaller havens of the Bristol Channel; it has served as a valuable reference in the process of compiling and cross-checking the *Bristol Channel and Severn Pilot*.

My thanks to Joyce and Jack Cumberlidge for their help in combing the text for errors, inaccuracies or inconsistencies.

Barry Harbour

Glossary of Admiralty Charts

Small-scale, for passage-planning

BA no. Title
1178   Approaches to the Bristol Channel
1179   Bristol Channel

Medium-scale

BA no. Title
1478   St Govan's Head to St David's Head
1076   Linney Head to Oxwich Point
1165   Worm's Head to Watchet
1152   Watchet to Weston-super-Mare and Barry to Newport
1176   Severn Estuary—Steep Holm to Avonmouth, including Newport
        and Redcliff Bay
1166   River Severn—Avonmouth to Sharpness
1164   Hartland Point to Ilfracombe, including Lundy
1156   Trevose Head to Hartland Point
1149   Pendeen to Trevose Head

Large-scale, including harbour plans

BA no. Title
2878   Approaches to Milford Haven
3274   Milford Haven—St Ann's Head to Newton Noyes Pier
3275   Milford Haven—Milford Dock to Picton Point
1482   Plans on the coast of SW Wales, including Tenby and Saundersfoot
        with approaches
1167   Burry Inlet
1161   Swansea Bay
1169   Approaches to Porthcawl
1182   Barry and Cardiff Roads with approaches, including Barry Docks
        and Cardiff Docks
1859   Port of Bristol, including King Road, River Avon and City Docks
1160   Plans on the coast of Somerset and Devon, including Ilfracombe,
        Lynmouth, Porlock, Minehead, Watchet, Barnstable and Bideford
1168   Harbours on the north coast of Cornwall, including Newquay Bay,
        approaches to Padstow, St Ives Bay

9

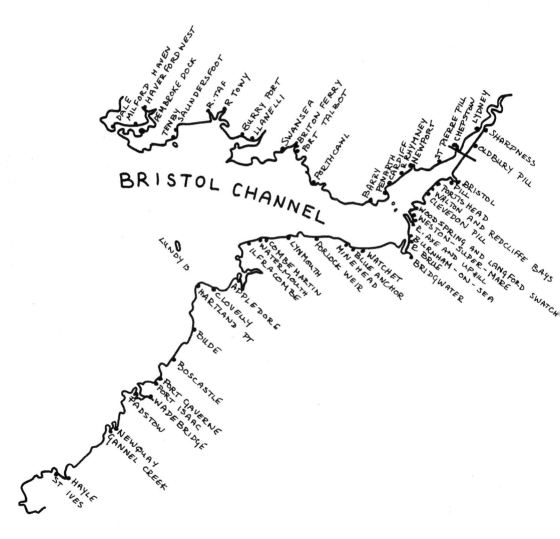

DALE
MILFORD HAVEN
HAVERFORD WEST
PEMBROKE DOCK
TENBY
SAUNDERSFOOT
R. TAF
R. TOWY
BURRY PORT
LLANELLI
SWANSEA
BRITON FERRY
PORT TALBOT
PORTHCAWL

BARRY
PENARTH
CARDIFF
R. RHYMNEY
NEWPORT
ST PIERRE PILL
CHEPSTOW
LYDNEY
SHARPNESS
OLDBURY PILL

BRISTOL
PILL
PORTIS HEAD AND REDCLIFFE BAYS
WALTON
CLEVEDON PILL
WOODSPRING AND LANGFORD
WESTON-SUPER-MARE
R. AXE AND UPHILL
BURNHAM-ON-SEA
R. BRUE
BRIDGWATER
SWATCH

BRISTOL CHANNEL

LUNDY IS

COMBE MARTIN
WATERMOUTH
ILFRACOMBE
LYNMOUTH
PORLOCK WEIR
MINEHEAD
BLUE ANCHOR
WATCHET

APPLEDORE
CLOVELLY
HARTLAND PT

BUDE

BOSCASTLE
PORT GAVERNE
PORT ISAAC
WADEBRIDGE
PADSTOW
NEWQUAY
GANNEL CREEK
HAYLE
ST IVES

Introduction to the Pilot

The Bristol Channel and Severn Pilot is the first published yachtsman's guide to concentrate its attention on that unique, tide-swept and fascinating cruising ground which lies between Wales and the West Country. For many years now, the only really comprehensive pilotage reference suitable for yachts has been the excellent, locally compiled 'Bristol Channel Yachting Conference Handbook', but the most recent edition of these useful notes was printed in 1980 and looks like being the last.

This new Pilot covers a much larger area than that included on the Admiralty chart of the Bristol Channel (BA 1179). In fact the scope of the book extends to all tidal waters to the east of a straight line joining St Ann's Head on the Welsh side (the west headland of Milford Haven entrance) and Pendeen Point on the Cornish side. The Pilot works eastwards along the north shore of the Bristol Channel, from Milford Haven right up to Lydney, and then westwards along the south shore, from Sharpness to St Ives.

Each port has its own section, organised in a way which it is hoped will make it easy to locate any required piece of information. Each section begins with a brief summary of the port, so that the navigator can hopefully obtain an instant picture of the sort of place he is dealing with, i.e. whether it is a deep water or drying harbour, when it can safely be entered, how sheltered it is, where to lie, and so on.

Immediately after each summary are the tide times and the local heights above chart datum. The times of local high water have been given as differences on both HW Dover and HW at the nearest standard port. Where applicable, port control VHF listening and working channels have been included after the tide times.

Bearings of marks ashore have been given from seaward, according to normal practice, but are generally in degrees magnetic rather than degrees true. While it is appreciated that variation is slowly changing, I have usually found that the consistent use of magnetic bearings makes life simpler aboard a small yacht, especially when you have stopped plotting on the chart and have, so to speak, reached the map-reading stage.

Each port generally has a separate heading for 'Entry at Night' and I have opted to include the more important light characteristics within the text. It seems to me that the convenience of having them to hand outweighs, on balance, any possible complications caused by the information going out of date. You should, in any case, always check lights as given in the Pilot against those in the most recent Admiralty List of Lights, or in one of the lists given in the various Almanacs. By the same token, the entry directions assume that the

11

navigator has in front of him the latest and largest scale Admiralty Chart.

The sketch charts in the Pilot are only intended as a guide to navigation and are not drawn completely to scale, but many of them give information which is more up to date and detailed than the Admiralty can supply. The smaller havens in the Bristol Channel are often buoyed by courtesy of the local yacht clubs, and in such cases their members have played an important part in drawing up the sketch charts and verifying their accuracy. However, I will always be grateful to receive any corrections from local or cruising yachtsmen, by letter or postcard c/o The Editor, Stanford Maritime.

The photographs have been chosen to be informative and also to give a feel for the character of each harbour. I have tended to steer clear of views from seaward, since I have usually found them of rather limited value in my own pilotage. One's visibility and distance off never quite seem to match those of a published photograph taken from a heaving deck!

While I have been cautious with entry directions, I've also tried not to write off the more tortuous entrances by including too many gloomy provisos. Almost anywhere is easy to get into near high water, given settled weather and light offshore winds, but even the trickiest Bristol Channel havens are used by local boats in a wide range of weathers. In the end, though, navigators must always trust their own judgement when deciding which places are safe to enter in *their* boats under the existing conditions.

Cruising in the Bristol Channel

It is probably fair to say that, until quite recently, yachtsmen have tended to regard the Bristol Channel as a rather hostile stretch of sea, whose strong tides and shifting sandbanks were not exactly conducive to relaxing cruising. Perhaps they had a point. It is certainly true that the Bristol Channel has some of the most powerful tides in Europe—the range at Avonmouth exceeds 13 metres at springs, and rates of over 6 knots are not uncommon. Nor can it be denied that the frequent patches of overfalls and swirling eddies are apt to create a somewhat malevolent impression, particularly in the upper reaches. It is also the case that many of the harbours dry out, offering only limited shelter, a risk of swell, and no special facilities for visitors.

But the great thing about cruising in the Bristol Channel is that it is unspoilt in the best sense of the word. Here, in this fascinating gulf between Wales and the West Country, you can experience cruising as it once was, before the relentless provision of 'facilities' began to remove some of the magic from finding your way around in your own boat. The various havens described in this book, however small or tucked away, each have their own band of loyal enthusiasts, who often form a club to organise moorings and maintain the local navigation marks which are so necessary for some of the more tortuous entrances.

Not that things are completely untamed, thank heavens. There are now some excellent and strategically placed marinas in the Bristol Channel, so that yachtsmen can sample the best of both worlds and feel reasonably secure in the knowledge that a sheltered bolt-hole is not too far away. However independent your style of cruising, it is always good to be able to pull into civilisation from time to time, top up with fuel and water, have a hot shower and enjoy an uninterrupted night's rest.

Although the Channel represents a substantial cruising area, it can sometimes seem compact, partly because the strong tides tend to reduce passage times and partly because, except at the 'Atlantic' end, you can usually see across from shore to shore. There is also a considerable diversity in both landscape and seascape.

On the Welsh side, starting in the west, you have the long sheltered estuary of Milford Haven which offers a self-contained cruising ground in its own right. From the entrance to the sheltered upper reaches of the Cleddau River is a good 15 miles, and it can take you weeks to discover all the nooks and crannies of the Haven. There is a good sheltered marina at Neyland, just opposite Hobbs Point, which makes a very pleasant base for local sailing.

Working east past St Govan's Head, you will come across green and pleasant Caldy Island, a monks' retreat which also serves as a natural outer breakwater for the harbours of Tenby and Saundersfoot. At the back of Carmarthen Bay, the wild Towy estuary is tricky to get into but worth the navigational effort involved. The outer channels wind between broad sandflats and the low shoreline can be extremely enigmatic as you approach from seaward. Further up the estuary are the dominating ruins of Llanstephan Castle, and Dylan Thomas's retreat at Laugharne.

About 10 miles from the mouth of the Towy lie the high cliffs and spectacular bays of the Gower Peninsula. Just north of the Gower is another rather difficult estuary, Burry Inlet, with the friendly harbour of Burry Port on its north side. The SE corner of the Gower terminates in Mumbles Head, with its familiar lighthouse and lifeboat slip. Now you are into Swansea Bay, with comfortable Swansea Yacht Haven not far to the north. This well-run marina was opened in 1983, the Bristol Channel's harbinger of 'decadence'.

Working east from Swansea, you cannot miss the straggling industrial complex at Port Talbot, with diminutive Porthcawl not far beyond. East of Nash Point the Bristol Channel becomes the Severn estuary and begins to narrow, and you reach the ports of Barry, Cardiff and Newport.

Just opposite Cardiff, Camper & Nicholsons have recently converted the old Penarth coal dock into a sheltered yacht harbour called Portway Marina, entered, as is Swansea Yacht Haven, by way of a sea-lock. Portway fills a natural gap on the north coast of the Bristol Channel and it is good to see the once bustling dock restored to a state of activity.

Above Penarth, what is now the River Severn needs treating with great respect. The tidal streams become fierce as the estuary narrows, and the sandbanks and rocky shoals seem more numerous and extensive. It is common enough for yachtsmen to take a professional Pilot above Avonmouth, although if you carefully follow the directions in this book you should not go far wrong.

From the docklands at Avonmouth and Bristol it is not far upstream to the imposing spans of the Severn Suspension Bridge, and thence to Lydney on the north shore and Sharpness on the south. At Sharpness you can lock into an interesting old dock and discover a quiet backwater of yacht moorings in the original entrance basin of the Sharpness to Gloucester Canal. This historic canal is still used commercially, and yachts can thus gain access to a considerable network of inland waterways. Above Gloucester the canalised Upper Severn leads on to Tewkesbury and the attractive old city of Worcester.

Back down at the western end of the Bristol Channel, the character of the English coastline is different yet again. You have picturesque St Ives, close to the rocky tip of Cornwall; secluded creeks such as the Gannel; or perhaps the restful Camel River. You can sample traditional Cornish fishing communities like Port Isaac, or friendly holiday towns such as Bude.

Sailing eastwards into Devon, past Lundy Island and Hartland Point, you come across the fascinating estuary of the Rivers Taw and Torridge. Here is the small but industrious shipbuilding town of Appledore, and the old market town of Bideford. The Torridge is not always easy to get into, but offers good shelter once you have crossed the bar and reached Appledore Pool. Ilfracombe is next up-Channel, one of the most secure havens on this coast. Then on past Lynmouth and Porlock Weir to Minehead and Watchet, and thence to the rather bleak approaches to Burnham-on-Sea and the new marina at Bridgwater.

Weston-super-Mare is well known for its holiday beaches, but it also has a small pier harbour. A couple of miles to the south, right in the SE corner of Weston Bay, you can find the narrow mouth of the drying River Axe which has numerous local moorings and several sailing clubs. Between Weston and Portishead there are some quiet and rather unusual little hideaways such as Woodspring Bay, Langford Swatch and Clevedon Pill.

Portishead Dock is now practically disused, but there is an anchorage just outside in Portishead Pool. Then you are back to Avonmouth again, and where else in Europe will you find such a selection of ports-of-call as the Bristol Channel can provide?

But those who cruise these waters need to be well prepared in certain respects. The ability to take the ground easily and safely is a huge advantage, and will enable you to get the most out of Bristol Channel cruising. Not that keelboats cannot get around and see places too: legs can be used in certain harbours, and there are various anchorages where quite deep-draft boats can simply sit upright in soft mud.

Good-sized water tanks are a must, since there will not be many opportunities to fill up from a convenient hose. The same applies to fuel. You really want to be able to carry a fortnight's supply of diesel, so that you are not committed to calling at one of the few harbours where it is easily available.

Tides rule your life in the Bristol Channel. The upper reaches have powerful streams and small yachts cannot make against them. Plan your passages in tidal legs, rather than in absolute mileage. When you are running out of favourable stream it is time to pull in somewhere, if only to a nearby anchorage.

Good ground tackle is absolutely essential. Ideally, you should carry a couple of heavy anchors and a good scope of sturdy chain for use in anger, and two lighter anchors with long nylon warps for rowing out in the dinghy. This can be quite common, such as when you have to moore fore-and-aft in a narrow 'pill', or when you go aground accidentally and need to lay out a kedge for when the tide returns. For the two main anchors I would choose a CQR and a fisherman's; for the lighter kedges, a second CQR and a Bruce.

A reliable echo-sounder is a must, but so is a lead-line. A sounder can give rogue readings under certain conditions that are not unusual in the Bristol Channel—a high concentration of suspended silt in a fast-flowing stream, underwater turbulence caused by powerful streams running over an uneven bottom, a layer of very soft mud over a rocky bottom— all of these can trick your echo-sounder into giving strange readings.

For extended Bristol Channel cruising your boat should be fairly self-sufficient in the way of tools and spare parts, because you might have to carry out running repairs in some isolated river or creek. Nor must you stint yourself over the question of large-scale charts. Admiralty charts are really the best bet for the Bristol Channel, since they are more likely to be up to date, and a full list is given on p. 151.

A powerful engine is an undeniable advantage, especially if you have only just missed a tide and can save the day by plugging against the early part of the foul stream. And yet, on the other hand, a good reserve of horsepower is by no means necessary. In a more civilised past, some of the smallest and seemingly most tortous havens in the Bristol Channel were used regularly by surprisingly large sailing coasters.

Take Porthcawl for example, a tiny pier harbour with a dogleg entrance and

15

a narrow gap between the breakwaters. Somehow or other, large, unhandy sailing cutters used to work their way in and out, heavily laden with coal and other cargoes. Over on the south coast, Watchet and Porlock Weir can seem difficult enough, even with 30hp of diesel engine poised under the cockpit sole. But the traders of the last century had no such luxury and seemed to manage pretty successfully.

For those who have not yet succumbed to the high-tech assistance of a Decca Navigator, a good RDF set can be worth its passage in poor visibility. There are not all that many radio beacons in the Bristol Channel, but it is not a huge area and the beacons which do exist are well placed.

Finally, don't be afraid to ask for local advice. The Bristol Channel has many small sailing and boating clubs, some of them in the most unlikely places. Each of these salty communities is a veritable mine of navigational knowledge, and by chatting with club members you can find out about recent changes in buoyage, sandbanks that have shifted slightly and channels that have changed their course. In compiling this pilot book I have drawn upon the expertise and experience of many local yachtsmen, though space has not allowed me to include all of what they had to say.

Once again, I would be very grateful to hear about any changes that may have occurred since this book was published, any inaccuracies which might have slipped through the net, or any new and relevant local knowledge that could usefully be included in a future edition. A short note or postcard to me, care of the Editor, Stanford Maritime, would be much appreciated.

Milford Haven

Summary An extensive natural harbour formed by the Cleddau estuary. There are several passage anchorages near the mouth and more sheltered berths, including a marina, further up-river. Entry is straightforward by day or night at any state of tide and the Haven makes a good port of refuge. Keep clear of large tankers in the harbour and approaches. The Cleddau is navigable by most yachts for 12 miles.

Tides HW Milford Haven is at HW Dover −5hr 00min. Heights above chart datum outside Milford Docks: 7.0m MHWS, 0.7m MLWS, 5.2m MHWN, 2.5m MLWN.

Port Control Milford Haven Port Authority. Call Milford Haven Signals Station on VHF Ch. 16 (working mostly on 12 and 14).

Tidal streams and currents

Off Milford Haven entrance the main Bristol Channel streams flow E by S and W by N; the E-going stream begins at local HW +04hr 55min and the W-going stream at local HW −01hr 00min. Both can reach 2–3 knots at springs. The flood in the entrance begins soon after local LW and reaches 1½ knots at springs; the ebb begins about ½hr after local HW and can reach 2 knots at springs. The streams in and out of the Haven often cause a confused sea where they meet the main flow of the Bristol Channel.

Rates in the Cleddau vary considerably, depending on the stretch of river, whether you are on the inside or outside of a bend, and how close you are to shoals. The streams are weaker above Lawrenny. In the lower reaches, near Pembroke Dock, the ebb can reach 4 knots locally at springs; the flood may reach $2\frac{1}{2}$–3 knots particularly when a fresh westerly is blowing up the river. HW at Lawrenny is approx. 15 min after HW Milford Haven, and the flood above Llangwm may run for $1\frac{1}{2}$ hr after HW Milford Haven.

Description

When you think of Milford Haven you probably imagine massive tankers, vast refineries and murky water. But the oil industry is only part of the story; much of the estuary is quite rural and the waters are invariably clear and unpolluted. Indeed, the Haven is a fine natural harbour which makes a fascinating place to visit for yachts. It is easy to access and there is plenty of sheltered river to explore. The entrance is about $1\frac{1}{2}$ miles wide and faces SSW between St Ann's Head and East Blockhouse Point. Inside these protecting headlands the drowned valley of the Cleddau turns E to provide a deep shipping channel up to Pembroke Dock.

Milford Haven developed as an oil port in the late 1950s and early '60s, although that boom has since turned into a gradual decline. The long jetties for the tanker berths reach out into the harbour, and ships are linked by a maze of pipes to refineries close inland. Strangely enough, these tangled complexes do not jar with the landscape; the grand scale of the estuary has somehow managed to absorb it all. The perpetually burning refinery flares cast an eerie glow as you come up the river at night.

In the lower reaches of the Haven the oil terminals restrict navigation mostly to the buoyed fairway, and yachts should not approach within 100m of jetties or tankers. Yet the upper Cleddau is quite unspoilt. The main options for visiting yachts are a reasonable anchorage at Dale, the Westfield Marina at Neyland, and visitors' moorings off Hobbs Point and Lawrenny Quay.

Looking downstream past the entrance to Milford Docks. In the background are the Amoco and Esso oil terminals, with Thorn Island and the entrance to the Haven beyond.

Outer approaches

Coming from seaward, the principal danger is the Turbot Bank, 4 miles S of St Ann's Head and marked by a W-cardinal buoy. The Bank can kick up a nasty sea in fresh winds, particularly when the tide is weather-going, so give the area a wide berth under these conditions.

Approaching from the E along the coast in moderate weather, the shortest route is between St Govan's Head race and the overfalls over St Gowan Shoals. Keep about 1½ miles off the headland, especially on the ebb stream in a W wind. Although the shoals have a least depth of 6m, the sea often breaks over them and tide rips may extend up to 5 miles E. As you near Milford Haven give the rocks off Linney Head a good berth.

MOD firing range On weekdays during the summer there is usually practice firing in the range between St Govan's Head and Linney Head. If approaching this area you can expect to be hailed by one of the patrol launches or called on VHF Ch 16, and directed some miles offshore. To avoid such a detour stay a good 5 miles off in the first instance, outside the St Gowan LtV. For times of firing telephone Castlemartin 262 or Manorbier 281.

Approaching Milford Haven from the W, avoid Wildgoose Race just W of Skomer and Skokholm, by keeping about 2 miles seaward of both islands. Further out, note that overfalls can extend to over a mile SE of Grassholm island.

Entry

In daytime with good visibility Pennar power station chimney can be identified from up to 25 miles offshore. St Ann's Head forms the W arm of Milford Haven entrance, a flat-topped promontory with a conspicuous white lighthouse and cluster of Coastguard buildings at its S tip. On the E side of the entrance is East Blockhouse Point, with Sheep Island ½ mile S of it.

Milford Haven entrance

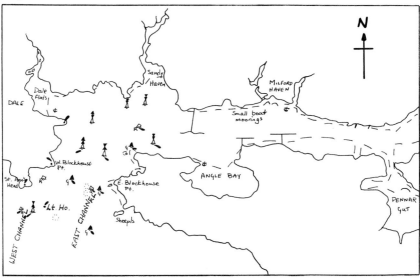

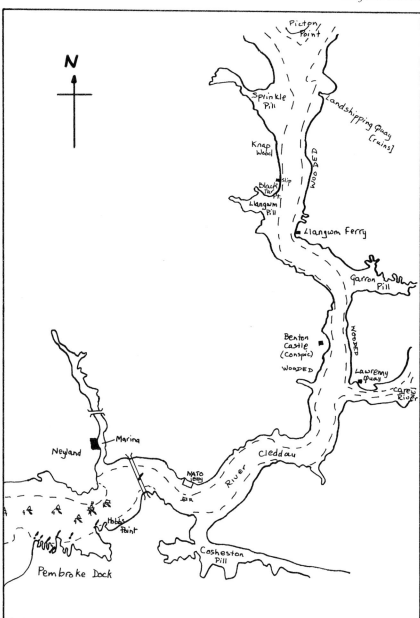

Milford Haven, upper reaches

There is plenty of room to work into the Haven under sail; both shores are steep-to and yachts need not keep to the buoyed channels. However, Middle Channel Rocks (with 5m over them) and Chapel Rocks (with 3m) should both be avoided in heavy weather. The leading marks on Great Castle Head and Little Castle Head provide a useful reference.

There are two buoyed shipping channels into the Haven. West Channel is entered $\frac{1}{2}$ mile S of St Ann's Head, between St Ann's red can buoy and Middle Channel Rocks W-cardinal buoy which is close SW of Middle Channel Rocks lighthouse. From this gate West Channel leads 048°Mag. as far as Angle N-cardinal buoy. The fairway then turns E and is well marked up to Hobbs Point.

East Channel is entered a little over $\frac{1}{2}$ mile WSW of Sheep Island, leaving the Sheep green conical buoy close to starboard. Thereafter the buoyed channel trends NNE and N as far as Thorn Rock W-cardinal. Although West Channel is the deeper of the two, East Channel can be a better bet in strong southwesterlies, particularly during gales when the ebb is running. Under these conditions a confused and sometimes dangerous sea builds up in the vicinity of the ledges SW of St Ann's Head. **Caution**: if you are using the East Channel you may see local fishing boats cutting between Thorn Island and Thorn Point. This passage saves no great distance, and the overhead cables which supply power to the island's small hotel only give a least headroom of 15ft at MHWS.

Once inside the entrance follow the buoyed fairway more or less, but remember that yachts can use large areas of water outside the buoys. Indeed it is often safer as well as considerate to stay out of the main channel when tankers are under way. Keep well clear of oil jetties, the many large mooring buoys and any manoeuvring ships and tugs. The byelaws give right of way to commercial traffic.

Milford Haven town and docks are situated on the N bank just beyond the Amoco terminal. Having passed Milford and the Texaco terminal opposite, keep over to the N side of the river. Off the S shore, the shoal area known as Pwllcrochan Flats dries at LAT to well over half the width of the Cleddau—visitors are apt to disbelieve the chart at this point! Beyond Pwllcrochan, work southwards to leave Wear Spit beacon to port. The channel then follows the N shore again past Carr Rocks and Dockyard Bank.

Entry at night

The West Channel is better lit than the East. St Ann's Head light has a 23M

The Upper Cleddau and the channel to Haverfordwest

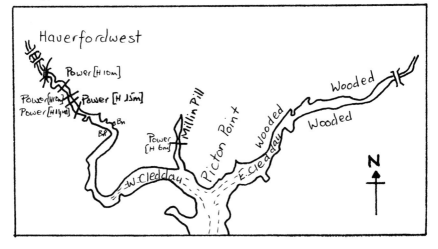

range (FlWR, 5s); a red sector covers St Gowan Shoals to the SE and the intense red covers the unlit rocks off Linney Head. Middle Channel lighthouse has a 12M range (Fl3G, 7s). Approach from the SSW with St Ann's Head white sector to port and Middle Channel light to starboard. The first set of leading lights bearing 030°Mag. brings you in as far as Middle Channel W-cardinal buoy; the front light is on West Blockhouse Point (FWR) and the rear light on Watwick Point (FW).

The second set of leading lights then takes you into the Haven; the front light is on Great Castle Head (Occ 4s) and the rear light on Little Castle Head (Occ 8s). Follow this transit, bearing 048°Mag., to just beyond Angle N-cardinal buoy. Then turn E along the well lit fairway that leads up the harbour, or head NW to round Dale Point (Fl2WR, 5s) if you are bound for the Dale anchorage. In the latter case note the Dakotian E-cardinal buoy (QF3, 10s) 3½ cables E of Dale Point, which marks a wreck with 1.9m over it. Also watch out for two large MOD mooring buoys, one about 3 cables NE of Dale Point and the other about 2 cables due S of the Dakotian, lit by faint yellow flashing lights. They also have triple-span mooring chains and anchoring is not advisable within 200m.

To enter the East Channel at night, first make for the Sheep buoy and then follow the fairway as by day. Once inside Thorn Island it is preferable to stay within the buoyed channel in order to avoid the numerous large, unlit mooring buoys in the Haven.

There are often several small tankers anchored in Dale Roads, with bright and confusing deck lights. This can make it difficult to pick out some of the inner navigation marks from the outer approaches between St Ann's Head and Sheep Island. Keep in mind, however, that the pilotage into the Haven is not at all critical, and the lights will become clear as you get further in.

Berths and anchorages

Dale   The village lies near the mouth of Milford Haven, at the head of an attractive bay just inside the entrance on the W side, and it offers a convenient passage anchorage in westerly weather. You can stay afloat at all states of tide so long as you bring up well outside the local moorings; the silty sand bottom shoals towards the village. Take careful soundings as you come in and before you settle down for the night.

In southwesterlies, anchor off the S shore close under the steep-to arm of Dale Point. If there is much north in the wind, tuck under the opposite shore for shelter. Avoid Dale in easterlies, when there's a longish fetch across the lower reaches of the Haven. Dale Flats, the inlet NW of the moorings, dries out to stony mud and is only suitable for bilge or lifting keel boats. Land at the beach near the Dale Yacht Club. The members welcome visiting yachtsmen and if the clubhouse is not open the key can be obtained from the Dale Sailing Co., who have a chandlery and boatyard on the front. There are shops nearby in the village.

Sandy Haven   A couple of miles E across the Haven from Dale is Sandy Haven Bay, at the head of which is Sandy Haven itself, a secluded wooded creek which makes a perfect hideaway for shallow draft boats that can take the ground. Deeper draft yachts can anchor near the creek mouth over a sandy bottom, as tide permits. In northwesterlies there is a good spot about 2 cables NE of Little Castle Head in about 1.5m.

The moorings and anchorage off Dale makes a handy stopover if you are on passage and don't want to go right up the Haven to Westfield Marina or Hobbs Point.

Be careful to avoid Bull Rock (dries 1.5m) a cable E of Little Castle Head, and some other rocky patches about 2 cables NE of Bull Rock. Clear out of this outer anchorage if the wind shifts to S.

Angle Bay   A wide, shallow inlet on the S side of the Haven directly opposite the Esso and Amoco terminals. It is entered between Angle Point and Sawdern Point and a large refinery dominates the E shore. Although most of Angle Bay dries to soft mud, there are some local moorings in the NW corner just opposite the Old Point House inn; at neaps, yachts of moderate draft can stay afloat close to the E of these moorings. Shoal draft boats can take the ground at anchor, but note that parts of the foreshore around the bay are rocky.

Keep to the W side on the approach to Angle Bay, cutting close to the disused slipway on Angle Point. Thus you will avoid Buoy Rocks and Middle Rocks in the mouth of the bay, two drying rocky patches which are unmarked. Angle is a sheltered spot in westerlies but is open to the N. The village is a short walk away along the beach.

Near LWS it will not be possible to stay afloat in Angle Bay, but there is a deep-water anchorage over sand, close off the S shore of the Haven anywhere up to $\frac{1}{2}$ mile W of Angle Point. There is reasonable shelter here in winds between SW through S to SE.

Milford Haven town   A pleasant enough place, with reasonable rail connections eastwards via Swansea. However the docks are not all that convenient for yachts, access being by way of a lock worked from 2 hr before until HW. Contact Milford Docks Radio in advance on VHF Ch 9, 12, 14 or 16. Entry signals are shown from the E side of the gate: a blue flag by day and two green vertical lights at night. If you are early on the tide bear in mind that the approaches to Milford are fairly shallow. The narrow buoyed channel is dredged to 2.9m.

Anchoring off Milford is not ideal, although at neaps you can lie in the

Camper and Nicholsons Westfield Marina at Neyland, immediately opposite the Hobbs Point landing slip. The marina is very sheltered and makes a convenient base for local cruising.

shallows over Milford Shelf about 4 cables SE of the lock entrance. The area is rather exposed to the SW and there is often a persistent swell, but the shelter is OK in northerlies. Local moorings are laid off Hakin Point and you can usually find a vacant buoy for an hour or so. In Gelliswick Bay, ½ mile W of Hakin Point, there is a fair weather neap anchorage off the Pembrokeshire YC slipway; the bay dries out to sand at LAT.

Pennar Gut   Anchor just inside the mouth of this shallow inlet in about 4m, 2 cables due S of East Pennar Point. There is good shelter except in northerlies, though the power station makes a rather gloomy backdrop. The narrow channel into Pennar Gut is marked by an unlit red can buoy off the S shore of the Haven a mile or so WSW of Pembroke Dock. Landing is not permitted at the power station jetty.

Hobbs Point   On the S side of the Cleddau, about 7 miles above the mouth of the Haven and just below the road bridge. There is a quay and a wide slipway, but only temporary berthing alongside. Pembroke Haven YC is set back from the quay, and Kelpie Boats' chandlery and diesel fuelling berth are next to the slip (tel (0646) 683661, VHF Ch 37(M) and 16). Kelpie maintains a number of visitors' moorings between Hobbs Point and the bridge, reasonably sheltered from SW through S to E.

Westfield Marina   This recent development of Camper & Nicholson has involved dredging Westfield Pill, a narrow creek on the N side of the river directly opposite Hobbs Point. Over 200 pontoon berths have been established in two basins; the upper basin has a sill whereas the lower one is accessible at any state of tide. The sill has a tide gauge at either side, and has 5m depth at MHW.

A dredged channel leads into the creek, marked by two port and two starboard hand buoys; it carries a least depth of 2m at LAT. Pass outside the old pier stagings on entry and not through the small-boat mooring area N of these stagings. About 30 visitors' berths are normally available during the season and they are sheltered from all quarters. Use the outer pontoons first, unless directed otherwise. The maximum length that can be accommodated is 80ft; the maximum draft is 2.0m in the lower basin at lowest springs, and slightly more in the upper basin.

The marina maintains a 24 hr listening watch on Ch 37(M), or you can telephone them on Neyland (0646) 601601. Specialist services ashore include hauling out, storage, hull and engine repairs, chandlery, diesel, also petrol with prior notice; contact the Dale Sailing Co. on (0646) 601636.

Lawrenny Yacht Station 2½ miles above Westfield Pill the Cresswell and Carew Rivers flow into the Cleddau from the E. On the N shore of this confluence is the Lawrenny Yacht Station (tel (064 67) 212), a kind of nautical country park which has some deep-water moorings, a chandlery and a small boatyard with a slip. Diesel is available alongside the quay. The moorings are sheltered, the surroundings attractively rural and the Lawrenny Arms Hotel is close by. This is a good place to stop if you plan to explore the upper reaches of the Cleddau.

The Upper Cleddau The peaceful and unspoilt upper stretches of the river offer various anchorages depending on your draft. A good deep-water spot is just opposite Lawrenny in Castle Reach, presumably named after Benton Castle, conspicuous on the W bank high among the oaks. Castle Reach turns into Beggars Reach at the mouth of Garron Pill, and then you come up with the picturesque village of Llangwm. There is a pleasant anchorage off Llangwm Pill and a landing slip at Black Tar Point.

There are no navigation buoys or perches in these higher reaches, so use the large-scale Admiralty chart 3275. Off Black Tar Point the river is relatively deep and narrow, and there are some moorings close under Knap Wood. Then a broad mud flat pushes the fairway over to the E past the ruins of Landshipping Quay, and the river divides at Picton Point. More moorings are laid in the lower part of the East Cleddau, where there is limited room to anchor.

The peaceful moorings off Lawrenny Quay, where the Cresswell and the Carew Rivers meet.

Tenby Harbour is one of the most attractive ports of call on the South Wales coast. Visitors berth alongside the inner wall of the breakwater, drying out on firm sand. Castle Hill and the lifeboat slip can be seen in the background.

The West Cleddau leads for another 3 miles up to the old market town of Haverfordwest. The channel is shallow and unmarked, and should only be negotiated by boats up to 1.2m draft that can take the ground easily, preferably on the last of the flood. The banks close in considerably above Hook. Four sets of high-voltage power cables span the river on the outskirts of Haverfordwest, with clearance heights between 10 and 15m; these dictate the limit of navigation for most sailing yachts. Motor boats can almost reach the town, but the channel vanishes to a trickle among the reeds and there's no convenient place to berth.

Tenby

Summary One of the most attractive havens on the South Wales coast, huddled in the SW corner of Carmarthen Bay 2 miles N of Caldey Island. Easy to approach, it makes a useful staging point between Milford Haven and Swansea. The small harbour is accessible about $2\frac{1}{2}$ hr either side of HW, dries to firm sand and is sheltered from most quarters, although fresh winds between NE and SE tend in a swell. Visiting yachts lie alongside the breakwater inner wall, close to the town. There is an outer anchorage 2–3 cables NNE of the lifeboat slip, sheltered from NW through W to SSW.

Tides HW Tenby is at HW Milford Haven −00hr 10min, or HW Dover −5hr 10min. Heights above chart datum: 8.4m MHWS, 0.9m MLWS, 6.3m MHWN, 3.0m MLWN.

Port Control Tenby Borough Council. HM tel Tenby (0834) 2717, VHF listening watch on Ch 16 during office hours.

Tidal streams and currents

NE of the harbour in Tenby Roads streams barely reach a knot at springs. Stronger rates occur between Tenby and Caldey Island; $1\frac{1}{2}$ knots at springs in Caldey Roads and up to 3 knots in Caldey Sound. In Caldey Sound the ebb flows WSW from 1 hr before to 4 hr after HW Tenby, and ENE from 5 hr after to 2 hr before HW.

Description

Tenby is a popular seaside town which has managed to retain much of its traditional charm. Facing broadly E across Carmarthen Bay, quaint terraced houses look down across a small, drying harbour towards the sheltering promontory of Castle Hill and its lifeboat slip. St Catherine's Island with its old fort lies close SE of Castle Hill and is connected to it by a drying ridge of sand. From the harbour breakwater, on a clear day, you can see across Carmarthen Bay to the high ground of the Gower Peninsula. A couple of miles S of Tenby Roads anchorage is the green and pleasant monastic retreat of Caldey Island.

The harbour dries to firm sand, joining with North Beach at LW. The local moorings are closely laid and visitors normally take the ground alongside the breakwater inner wall; there are ladders and it is handy for the town. The harbour is liable to swell in any E wind, although Castle Hill and the breakwater protect Tenby from direct onslaught. The approaches are straightforward, but Woolhouse Rocks (drying 3.6m) lie $1\frac{1}{4}$ miles SE of Castle Hill. Tenby Roads are shallow and the outer anchorage is a good $\frac{1}{4}$ mile NE of the breakwater at springs.

Tenby Sailing Club welcome visitors at their premises on the W quay. Fuel is not available near the harbour and involves a fair hike with a jerry-can, though there is a chandler in town and water at the breakwater. The railway connects with Carmarthen and thence E or W via the main coast line.

Outer approaches

When approaching Tenby from the westward, Caldey Sound is the most direct route—given daylight and moderate weather. Enter from the WSW between Lydstep Point and St Margaret's Island, steering for Giltar Point and leaving St Margaret's at least 2 cables off. Note Lydstep Ledge (2.8m) just over $\frac{1}{2}$ mile E of Lydstep Point, and Sound Rock (4.2m) a cable further E; there are overfalls in the vicinity of these two shoals in a weather-going tide.

Caldey Sound carries a least depth of 3m in the buoyed channel. Pass between Giltar Spit red can buoy and Eel Point green conical buoy, and then head NE keeping Eel Point buoy just open of Caldey Island astern to avoid the NE extremity of Giltar Spit. When North Highcliff N-cardinal buoy bears roughly SSE and Tenby promenade begins to open up behind Castle Hill, alter to the N for Tenby Roads. Leave Sker Rock, off St Catherine's Island, a cable to port.

At night, pass S of Caldey Island staying at least $\frac{1}{2}$ mile off in a weather-going tide. Heavy overfalls can occur up to $\frac{1}{2}$ mile SW of West Beacon Point. Drift Rock (9.8m) is $1\frac{1}{4}$ miles SE of Chapel Point and the W-going tidal stream can kick up a nasty sea in its vicinity. Spaniel Shoal (3m) lies $\frac{1}{2}$ mile E of

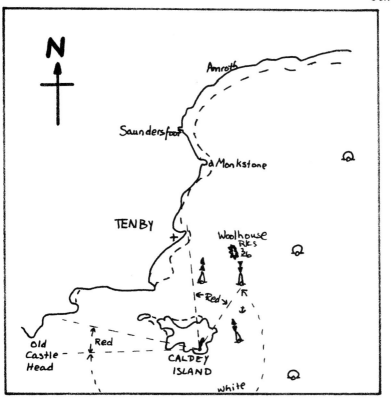

Approaches to Tenby and Saundersfoot

Tenby

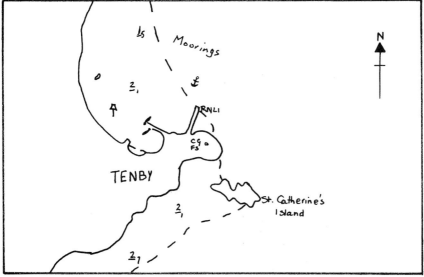

Caldey, and yachts can normally pass either side of the Spaniel E-cardinal buoy.

Woolhouse Rocks, drying 3.6m, lie 1¼ miles NE of Caldey Island. Avoid Woolhouse, either by staying close to the E of North Highcliff N-cardinal buoy, or else by skirting well to the E of Woolhouse S-cardinal buoy.

Approaching Tenby from the E, say from Burry Inlet, make directly for Castle Hill by keeping Tenby church spire just open N of St Catherine's Island. This line passes close N of DZ2 yellow spherical buoy and leaves Woolhouse Rocks ½ mile to the S.

Coming from the SE round the Gower Peninsula, either make for the E side of Caldey Island and thence to Castle Hill via the North Highcliff buoy, or else head up for DZ2 yellow spherical buoy and come N-about Woolhouse Rocks. Approaching from the ENE and the Towy estuary, head straight into Tenby Roads by making for the N side of Castle Hill.

Entry

Having reached Tenby Roads, approach the harbour from the NE giving a good clearance to the end of the lifeboat slip. Head first for an iron beacon post standing on an isolated drying rock about 150m NW of the breakwater head. A similar distance NNW of this post is the conspicuous Gosker Rock, an islet close off North Beach. As the harbour begins to open up turn to port round the breakwater and come alongside its inner wall.

Entry at night

Since Caldey Sound is unlit, the night approach to Tenby from the W must be seaward of Caldey Island. Caldey lighthouse (Fl3WR, 20s) has two red sectors; one covering West Beacon Point and its off-lying ledges and the other covering Woolhouse Rocks.

Having rounded Chapel Point, Caldey's southern tip, head NNE for DZ2 yellow spherical buoy (FlY, 2.5s), keeping in the white sector of Caldey light.

The final approach to Tenby harbour from Tenby Roads. There is an anchorage outside the harbour in The Pool, 2–3 cables NNE of the lifeboat slip and sheltered from NW through W to SSW.

Note that Spaniel, North Highcliff and Woolhouse buoys are all unlit. From DZ2, make good 290°Mag. for Tenby Roads and the N side of Castle Hill. Keep a good lookout for boats moored or anchored in the Roads. Tenby breakwater head has fixed red and white lights.

Coming fiom the E or SE, make for the DZ2 buoy first, to be sure of passing Woolhouse Rocks to the N. Coming from the NE, make straight for the breakwater head lights.

Berths and anchorages

Tenby Harbour   Alongside the breakwater inner wall, drying out on firm sand. There is good shelter in most conditions, but easterly winds may send in a swell.

Tenby Roads   Anchor 2–3 cables NNE of the lifeboat slip. There is reasonable holding and good shelter in winds from NW through W to SSW, limited shelter from due S, but the anchorage is exposed to easterlies, particularly between E and SE.

Caldey Roads   Anchor in Priory Bay on the N side of Caldey Island, fair holding in sand. Keep clear of the ferry moorings but edge in as far as draft and tide permit. The anchorage offers reasonable shelter from SE through S to WSW, although it is rarely calm.

Jones Bay   There is an attractive temporary anchorage in Jones Bay, on the NE corner of Caldey Island, sheltered from S through W to NW. Tuck as close in as soundings allow.

Lydstep Haven   A wide sandy bay just N of Lydstep Point and a mile due W of Caldey Sound. The bottom is gradually shelving sand and the bay offers good shelter from the W. Edge as far in as draft and tide allow.

Saundersfoot

Summary   Just over 2 miles N of Tenby, in the NW corner of Carmarthen Bay. This small seaside town is not so picturesque as Tenby and tends to become more crowded with tourists. The enclosed harbour is accessible about 2 hr either side of HW, dries to firm sand and is protected from all quarters, although prolonged easterly winds send in a surge. The harbour is safe but usually full of local boats and has limited space for visitors. Berth alongside the SE breakwater inner wall, or the N wall immediately to starboard on entry. The outer anchorage is further offshore than at Tenby, but well sheltered from NNE through W to SSW.

Tides   HW Saundersfoot is at HW Milford Haven −00hr 10min, or HW Dover −5hr 10min. Heights above chart datum: 8.4m MHWS, 0.9m MLWS, 6.3m MHWN, 3.0m MLWN.

Port Control   Saundersfoot Harbour Commissioners. For HM tel Saundersfoot (0834) 3313.

Tidal streams and currents

Streams in the NW part of Carmarthen Bay are weak, barely reaching a knot at springs.

Description

Saundersfoot is a small seaside town on the NW side of Carmarthen Bay. The coastline to the N and E is renowned for its wide, sandy beaches and the whole area is popular with holidaymakers during the season. From a yachtsman's point of view, Saundersfoot's enclosed harbour is a safe haven once you are inside, although it is usually chock-a-block with local boats. The bottom dries out to firm sand and visitors usually lie alongside one of the quays. Saundersfoot Sailing Club have a pleasant clubhouse situated on the W side of the harbour.

The town is near the harbour, with good shopping, although it is best to get there early in the morning before most of the tourists are up and about. There is fresh water, a boatyard and chandlery on the quay. Fuel is not available alongside, but there is a garage in town. The railway station is on the same branch as Tenby, connecting with Carmarthen and thence E or W via the main coast line.

Outer approaches

As for Tenby, except that you have to work N into Carmarthen Bay for a further 2 miles. Between Tenby and Saundersfoot, give Monkstone Point a berth of at least $\frac{1}{4}$ mile since underwater rocks extend SE for 1 cable from the Monkstone itself. Coming from the E, say from Ferryside, the coastline is straightforward once you have cleared Carmarthen Bar.

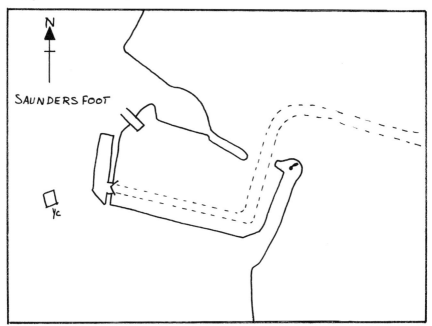

Saundersfoot

Entry

Enter or leave Saundersfoot within 2 hr of HW. Approach the SE breakwater head from due E, leaving a red can buoy marking a sewer outfall about a cable to port. When about 250m from the breakwater, curve NW towards a position 100m NNE of the entrance. Turn in towards the harbour when the entrance is fully open. Watch out for local fishing boats coming out, and leave the N breakwater head close to starboard on entry.

Entry at night

Straightforward once you have passed Monkstone Point, which is unlit. Coming from Tenby Roads, take back-bearings on the NE red sector of Caldey Island light (Fl3WR, 20s), until you have identified Saundersfoot breakwater light (FlR, 5s) and this bears less than about 310° Mag. Then head NNW until the breakwater light bears due W, distant $\frac{1}{2}$ mile, and proceed as above. The red can buoy marking the sewer outfall is unlit.

Berths and anchorages

Saundersfoot Harbour   Berth where you can find room, but first try either the SE breakwater inner wall or the N breakwater inner wall. If in doubt ask the Harbour Master, whose office is on the NW quay. There are sometimes one or two drying moorings available in the middle of the harbour.

Outer anchorage   In Saundersfoot Bay, $\frac{1}{2}$ mile SE of the harbour entrance at springs and about 3 cables offshore. At neaps, sound further inshore from the spring position. The holding is good in fine sand and the anchorage is sheltered from NNE through W to SSW. A riding light should be shown at night.

The Towy Estuary

Summary The Towy and Taf Rivers share a common estuary in the NE corner of Carmarthen Bay. The mouth is 2 miles wide, between Ginst Point and Tywyn Point, and the approaches are strewn with extensive drying sandbanks and a bar. The tide flows strongly through these dangers, which are largely unmarked, and the estuary is hostile in onshore winds. The few existing references advise strangers not to enter, except with local knowledge or a pilot. But it would be a pity to miss this wild, attractive stretch of water if conditions happened to be favourable. With careful pilotage, given light to moderate offshore winds and sufficient rise of tide, the estuary can be entered safely by boats of moderate draft that can take the ground. The drying anchorages off Ferryside a little way up the Towy, and at Laugharne up the Taf, are well worth the effort of navigation required to reach them.

Tides HW Ferryside is at HW Milford Haven −00hr 5min or HW Dover −05hr 05min. Heights above chart datum at Ferryside: 6.7m MHWS, 0.1m MLWS, 4.5m MHWN, 0.8m MLWN.

Port Control None. Members of the River Towy YC are sometimes listening on VHF Ch 16 and are pleased to advise on local conditions.

The River Towy Yacht Club landing stage at Ferryside, looking southwestwards towards Ginst Point and the mouth of the estuary.

Tidal streams and currents

Streams can be strong, both in the rivers and in the outer estuary. A spring flood may exceed 5 knots locally, especially across sandbanks and in the channel off Ferryside. Although neap tides make for more moderate rates, it is nonetheless preferable to plan a first visit near springs when there will be plenty of water over the shoals at HW. In any case strangers should not attempt to enter the Towy estuary until an hour before HW Ferryside, by which time the streams will have moderated.

Description

The Towy and Taf Rivers join and meet the sea in the NE corner of Carmarthen Bay, about 7 miles NW of the entrance to Burry Inlet. Either side of the mouth, dunes and burrows offer a rather featureless coastline to the navigator; much of this low-lying land is used as firing ranges by the Ministry of Defence. Like Burry Inlet, the Towy estuary is wide and shallow with extensive sandbanks making pilotage tricky and entry inadvisable in onshore winds. The sandbanks are continually shifting and the channel is not marked, but don't write off the estuary as a port of call. Both the Towy and the Taf are most attractive and completely unspoilt, and worth visiting if conditions permit. Gentle offshore winds and a moderate spring tide will allow strangers to enter safely. Follow the directions carefully and aim to cross Carmarthen Bar about an hour before local HW.

About 2 miles into the Towy on the E bank, the waterside village of Ferryside looks out across the river towards the imposing ruins of Llanstephan Castle. The River Towy Yacht Club's comfortable clubhouse is on the foreshore next to Ferryside station and a number of local boats are moored N of the landing stage, drying out about 2 hr either side of LW. The village has basic shopping and a garage which supplies diesel and petrol. The nearest chandlery and boatyard is at Burry Port.

Opposite Ferryside is Llanstephan village, just upstream from the castle. The river is shallower on this side, although you can still sound in towards the beach and take the ground. A mile above Llanstephan, past the River Towy Boat Club moorings, the Towy begins to narrow and shoal. Shallow draft boats can navigate as far as Carmarthen near HW, but masted boats can only reach the railway bridge $\frac{1}{2}$ mile below the town. Various high-tension electricity cables cross the river, with a least height of about 15m. It is best not to anchor in the upper reaches without local knowledge.

The Taf River is shallower than the Towy and joins the estuary just N of Ginst Point. The attractive village of Laugharne, where Dylan Thomas spent his last years, is 2 miles NW of Ginst Point. Here is another impressive ruined castle, and shoal-draft boats can dry out on the sand opposite Thomas's boathouse. The Taf is navigable on the tide by small craft almost as far as St Clears, 6 miles above the entrance.

The Towy Estuary and approaches to Ferryside

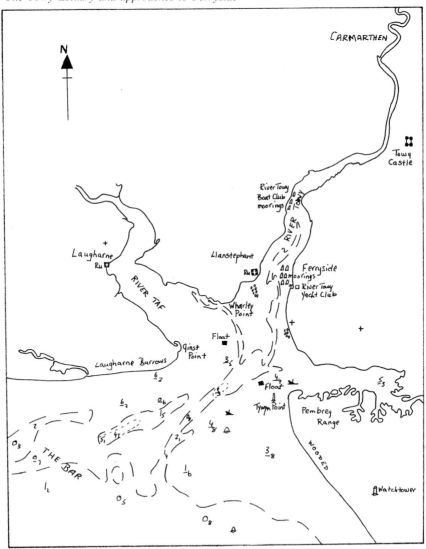

Outer approaches

Coming from the W up the Bristol Channel, enter Carmarthen Bay either by passing seaward of Caldey Island or by the inshore passage via Caldey Sound and Tenby Roads. Using the outer route, Carmarthen Bar lies 7 miles 055°Mag. from Spaniel E-cardinal buoy. By the inner route, the bar lies a similar distance 080°Mag. from the Tenby Roads anchorage.

Coming from the E round the Gower Peninsula, Carmarthen Bar lies 11 miles 330°Mag. from just off Worms Head, and nearly 13 miles 350°Mag. from Helwick LtV. Coming from Burry Inlet, Carmarthen Bar lies nearly 10 miles 315°Mag. from the entrance to South Channel.

Carmarthen Bay is largely clear of navigational dangers, but numerous yellow danger zone buoys mark areas used for Army and RAF artillery practice. A RAF safety craft patrols the Bay when firing is in progress and yachts may sometimes be asked to avoid particular zones. Permission is required to cross Pendine Range on the approach to the Towy estuary; intending visitors should contact the Pendine Range Controller, tel (099 45) 243 ext 240. There is usually no firing at weekends or during holiday periods.

Entry

At about an hour before HW Ferryside make a position just seaward of Carmarthen Bar, with Caldey Island lighthouse astern bearing 240°Mag. and distant 8 miles. This outer position is $1\frac{1}{2}$ miles off Pendine Burrows, with Ragwen Point bearing about 305°Mag.

Now make good 080°Mag., gradually closing the coast to within $\frac{3}{4}$ mile of Laugharne Burrows and heading towards the entrance of Gwendraeth Creek, just N of Tywyn Point. When the artillery range lookout tower on Ginst Point bears NNW, about a mile off, alter to the NE for St Ishmael church on the E side of the Towy River entrance. Make good 057°Mag. towards St Ishmael, keeping between two danger zone pontoons and making due allowance for the last of the flood tide setting in on your starboard quarter.

When about 4 cables off the church alter to 005°Mag. and head into the Towy for just over a mile, leaving an iron post beacon in mid-river about 50m to starboard. From here head NNE towards the River Towy Yacht Club landing stage; round up just beyond the landing in mid-stream, W of the local moorings.

To enter the River Taf, leave the westernmost of the danger zone pontoons about 3 cables to port and make good due N Mag. towards Wharley Point. When close under the point, alter to the WNW for Laugharne village, keeping roughly 200m off the N shore and fetching up about $\frac{1}{4}$ mile due E of Laugharne Quay.

Entry at night

On no account should strangers enter the Towy estuary at night, even in calm conditions. There are no navigation lights and there is no reliable way of locating the channel.

Berths and anchorages

Off Ferryside   Anchor in mid-river, a little way N of the River Towy Yacht

Local drying moorings at Ferryside, off the E shore of the River Towy. The best place to fetch up is over the sandbank shown here, a little way N of the yacht club landing stage and amongst the moorings.

Club landing stage and just W of the local moored boats. This should put you over a firm sandbank and away from the fast-flowing deeper water near the Ferryside shore. Good shelter from all quarters, but choppy in strong southerlies near HW. Land at the Club's stage.

Off Green Castle in Black Pool About $4\frac{1}{2}$ miles above Ferryside is Black Pool, a narrow stretch of river opposite Green Castle. Shoal-draft boats with local knowledge can anchor here in perfect shelter, having come up from Ferryside near HW. Visitors should first check with the yacht club as to the current depths and state of the bottom.

Off Laugharne Anchor about $\frac{1}{4}$ mile due E of Laugharne village over firm sand. Good shelter from all quarters. Land on the beach near Laugharne Quay.

Burry Port and Llanelli

Summary Burry Inlet, a wide, shallow estuary between the Gower Peninsula and the Dyfed coast, opens into the E side of Carmarthen Bay. It faces W, has a number of shifting sandbanks, and strangers can only enter safely in quiet weather near HW. Burry Port, on the N shore of the inlet, is a small drying harbour with about 200 local moorings. Passage above Burry Port is not recommended; Llanelli, 3 miles further up, can only offer two virtually derelict docks that dry. Neither harbour is suitable as a port of refuge.

Tides HW Burry Port is at HW Dover −4hr 55min, or HW Milford Haven −0hr 05min. Heights above chart datum: 7.8m MHWS, 0.9m MLWS, 5.8m MHWN, 3.0m MLWN.

Port Control Llanelli Borough Council, tel Llanelli (055 4) 758181. Harbour Superintendent, Mr Norman Hall is on duty 2 hrs either side of HW, tel Cross Hands (0269) 844315.

Tidal streams and currents

Streams in the estuary can be strong, reaching 4 knots at springs off Burry Port and over sandbanks. Off Burry Port the flood flows ENE until $\frac{1}{2}$ hr before local HW. There is then a short stand until about $\frac{1}{2}$ hr after HW, when the ebb begins to run WSW. Since depths in the approaches can vary as the sands shift, and because the streams often set across the channel, strangers should only approach or leave Burry Port during the last hour of the flood.

Description

Burry Inlet, which separates the Gower Peninsula from Dyfed, is the broad, shallow estuary of the Loughor River, whose sandbanks and shoals are continually shifting. The tide runs strongly through these dangers and the estuary is often written off by yachtsmen as being bleak and inhospitable. Yet the area has a rather haunting atmosphere and is worth a visit if weather and tides permit. The Gower itself offers rugged cliffs, striking headlands and wide, surf-washed bays of fine sand; its N shore is a wild region of drying flats, where horses graze the salt marshes and locals still gather cockles using donkey carts.

Burry Port lies nearly 5 miles NE of Burry Holms, a conspicuous islet off Limekiln Point at the NW corner of the Gower. Once a haven for small coasters, Burry Port had fallen into decline until quite recently but is now being revitalised for pleasure craft. There are about 200 drying moorings in the outer basin, some of them available for visitors.

The harbour has an unassuming charm, although its surroundings are rather run down. On the W quay are Burry Port Yacht Club, and Burry Port Yacht Services which has chandlery, can carry out engine and hull repairs and will arrange to deliver diesel or petrol. The club members welcome visitors. The town is only a short walk from the harbour and has reasonable shopping. A railway station provides connections W to Milford Haven and E via Swansea.

Outer approaches

Burry Inlet opens into the SE part of Carmarthen Bay, where the sandy bottom shelves gradually from seaward towards the mouth of the estuary. The passage across the bay from Saundersfoot or Tenby is straightforward, it being 15 miles ESE from Tenby harbour to Burry Holms. Ferryside to Burry Holms is a similar distance.

The entrance to Burry Inlet is complicated by the extensive shoals of Hooper and Pembrey Sands. These banks are continually shifting and even the latest Admiralty Chart (No 1167) is not so up-to-date as the sketch chart in this pilot book at the time of publication. Local knowledge is preferable for safe navigation, but Burry Port Yacht Club have recently laid some buoys which make the channels less elusive than hitherto.

Strangers will find the middle channel the simplest to locate, leaving Lynch

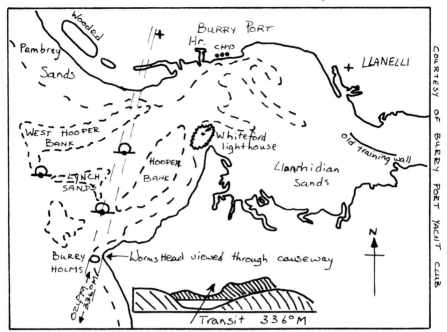

The following labels appear on the map:

Wooded

Pembrey

Sands

BURRY PORT
Hr.
CHYS

+ LLANELLI

WEST HOOPER
BANK

Whiteford
lighthouse

HOOPER
BANK

Llanrhidian
Sands

LYNCH
SANDS

old training wall

BURRY
HOLMS

Worms Head viewed through causeway

N

Transit 336°M

COURTESY OF BURRY PORT YACHT CLUB

Burry Inlet and the approaches to Burry Port

Sands to the W and Hooper Bank to the E. Therefore whether you are approaching from elsewhere in Carmarthen Bay or from further down the Bristol Channel, head for the S side of the estuary by first making a landfall on the high W coast of the Gower Peninsula, somewhere between Worms Head and Burry Holms.

In quiet weather there is a temporary anchorage, known as The Kitchen, close to the N of Worms Head; it is reasonably sheltered from due S or NE to E and the bottom is mostly sand. The Kitchen is useful if you are early on the tide for the estuary, but stay clear of the gap between Worms Head and Rhossili Point: the tide runs strongly through this narrow cut near half flood or ebb.

Entry

To enter Burry Inlet, aim to arrive not quite $\frac{1}{2}$ mile due W Mag of Burry Holms about an hour before HW. From here steer NE to leave Burry Holms $\frac{1}{4}$ mile to starboard and arrive at a position $\frac{1}{2}$ mile N by E of Burry Holms. Leave the first channel buoy close to port and, looking astern, bring Worms Head into view between Burry Holms and Limekiln Point, as shown in the Burry Inlet sketch chart. On this back-transit, make good about 024°Mag towards the right hand clump of trees on the distant skyline of Pembrey Mountain. This track will also leave the second channel buoy close to port.

Having passed this second buoy and with Whiteford lighthouse bearing due E Mag, make good 070°Mag for $1\frac{1}{2}$ miles and then head for the three conspicuous chimneys close E of Burry Port. Allow for the last of the flood tide setting you eastward and keep the left hand chimney bearing a little over 030°Mag. Identify Burry Port W breakwater, which has a low white

37

lighthouse with a red roof, but do not confuse this with the old Pembrey harbour breakwater, ½ mile further W.

Burry Inlet is a port of call for fine weather; unless you have local knowledge, only approach the estuary in light offshore winds. The mouth is unpleasant in moderate westerlies or southwesterlies, and heavy seas break across the entrance in fresh winds from these directions. It is not advisable to navigate the Inlet at night. If bound seawards from Burry Port, leave about ¾ hr before local HW.

The channel is tortuous above Burry Port, and dangerous in places where the strong tide could carry you over hidden obstructions. Local knowledge is necessary for the passage up to Llanelli, although the rather gloomy North Dock has little to tempt visitors. Beyond Llanelli the estuary narrows and becomes even more shoal, but small craft without masts can reach the Loughor Boating Club, situated just above the road bridge on the E bank.

Berths and anchorages

Burry Port Outer Harbour The harbour dries and has a level bottom of firm clay. The trot moorings are well maintained and are sheltered from all quarters, although strong winds from the S and SE send some swell into the harbour.

The Inner Harbours Visitors can use the E basin if there is room, entering near HW and drying out against the E wall or alongside another boat. The bottom here is soft mud, into which most craft sink without any trouble. The W basin is reserved for local boats.

Anchorage off Burry Port There is an anchorage off the harbour entrance in quiet weather, about 2 cables ENE of the spar beacon in 8–9m. You'll find moderate holding on a sandy bottom, strong currents and fair shelter from WNW through N to NE.

Llanelli Harbour Having first negotiated the difficult channel from Burry Port, yachts may berth in the old North Dock alongside one of the quays, entering near HW. They can also dry out on muddy sand alongside a quay in the narrow inlet just E of the dock entrance.

Lynch Pool There is a fair weather anchorage in Lynch Pool, over a sandy bottom close N of Limekiln Point in ½ to 3m LAT. This spot is open to the W, but reasonably sheltered from E through S.

The Gower Peninsula

From the land, the Gower Peninsula is an attractive, unspoilt holiday area which encompasses a variety of wild coastal scenery. The low tidal flats of the N shore contrast markedly with the dramatic cliffs and wide bays of the W and S. Yet the Gower can seem somewhat hostile from the yachtsman's point of

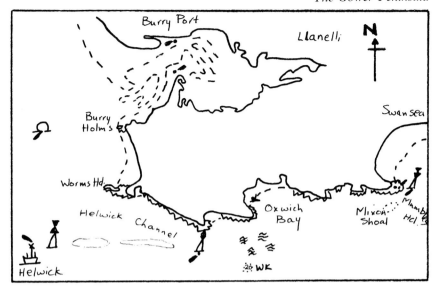

The Gower Peninsula

view. There are one or two quiet weather anchorages suitable for lunch and a swim, or for awaiting a fair tide, but the peninsula is generally rather exposed and it is usually wise to admire the many vistas while passing by as quickly as possible.

It is about 26 miles from Burry Port around the Gower to Swansea entrance, taking the best part of a tide under sail. There's a complication though, in that the E-going stream starts running off Worm's Head soon after local LW, whereas you have to leave Burry Port near HW. If weather permits, you can wait for the new flood at the Worm's Head anchorage: it is rarely worth pushing a foul tide S of the Gower. Coming from Tenby or Saundersfoot, leave about 2 hr after HW and allow for the weaker cross-tide of the ebb across Carmarthen Bay.

In moderate weather it is usually quicker to take the Helwick Channel inside Helwick Sands. This long, narrow shoal stretches due W for over 6 miles from just off Porteynon Point. Helwick Pass, the cut between Porteynon and the E end of the shoal, is marked by an E-cardinal buoy. West Helwick W-cardinal buoy guards the W end of the sands, and the Helwick LtV is moored about $1\frac{1}{2}$ miles SW of this buoy. Helwick Pass can be rough in fresh westerlies, or in any wind against the tide, the sea being steepest near LW.

Deep-draft yachts should only use Helwick Pass above half-tide. With less than 1.5m draft you can, in reasonable weather, aim to pass Worm's Head about an hour before local LW and so stem the last of the ebb down towards Porteynon Point. Helwick Pass will then be taken near LW and you'll arrive off Oxwich Point at slack when the overfalls are quiet. Be sure to avoid the wreck, with only 2.4m over it, 2 cables SE of Porteynon Point. In any fresh wind over tide conditions, clear Oxwich by 2 miles to miss the worst of the race.

There are pleasant daytime anchorages at Port Eynon and Oxwich bays, with reasonable shelter in light to moderate winds from WSW through N to

There is a useful anchorage in Mumbles Bay, about ¾ mile N of the lighthouse at springs but closer inshore at neaps. Local moorings are laid here and you will find reasonable shelter from N through W to SW, with good holding in stiff mud. Mumbles YC and the Bristol Channel YC have their premises ashore.

NE. Interestingly, a sizeable fishing fleet used to operate out of Port Eynon in the days of sail, and there was also a considerable limestone trade with Devon. There is no port now, but the Ship Inn still feels like a sailors' haunt.

Just over 6 miles ENE from Oxwich Point is Mumbles Head, with its famous lighthouse on the off-lying rocks and the well known pier and lifeboat slip round the corner to the N. Coming from the W, avoid Mixon Shoal (dries 0.7m), a small bank ¾ mile SSW of Mumbles lighthouse. An unlit red can buoy with bell is moored close S of this danger and should normally be left a good 2 cables to landward. Above half-tide in fine weather, yachts with good local knowledge can cut inside Mixon by keeping about 400m off the Coastguard station and a similar distance off the lighthouse, on the line of Oxwich Head to the Swigg S-cardinal buoy.

Once past Mixon bell-buoy Swansea Bay opens up, with Swansea harbour 4 miles to the NNE and the industrial complex of Port Talbot conspicuous to the E. Keep at least ¼ mile E of Mumbles lighthouse to avoid the Cherry Stones race and sewage outfall. There is a useful anchorage in Mumbles Bay, about ¾ mile N of the lighthouse at springs but closer inshore at neaps. You'll find reasonable shelter from N through W to SW, and good holding in stiff mud. Local moorings are laid here during the season, and both the Mumbles YC and the Bristol Channel YC have their premises ashore.

The Gower is especially inhospitable at night. The only lights are Helwick LtV (FlW, 10s, 26M), Mumbles Head (Fl4W, 10s, 17M), and two fixed red vertical lights on the end of Mumbles pier. Without local knowledge it is best to keep well offshore at night, staying outside Helwick LtV until Swansea opens up and you can begin to identify the harbour approach lights.

Swansea

Summary The city of Swansea is situated near the mouth of the River Tawe at the head of Swansea Bay. Swansea Yacht Haven, a modern marina with excellent facilities, is located on the W bank of the river ½ mile in from the harbour pierheads. Access to the marina is by way of a lock, worked for about

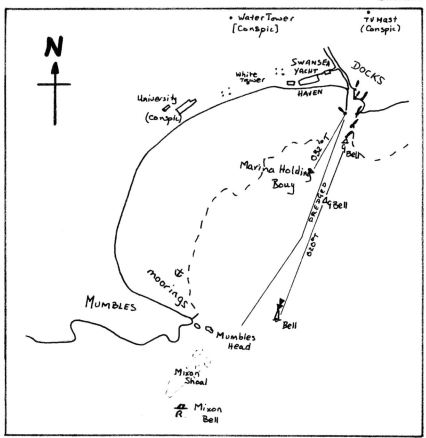

Approaches to Swansea Yacht haven

3 hr either side of HW during published hours. The Tawe approaches are well buoyed and entry is possible in practically all conditions of weather and tide.

Tides HW Swansea is at HW Dover −4hr 50min, i.e. at about the same time as HW Milford Haven. Heights above chart datum: 9.6m MHWS, 1.0m MLWS, 7.3m MHWN, 3.2m MLWN.

Port Control Swansea Dock Authority, VHF working Ch 14, with 24 hr listening watch on Ch 14 and 16. For marina call 'Swansea Yacht Haven' on Ch 37(M).

Tidal streams and currents

A mile or two S of Mumbles Head the E-going stream commences at approximately LW Swansea and the W-going stream at HW Swansea, with a maximum rate of about $2\frac{1}{2}$ knots at springs. A stronger local stream runs close past Mumbles pier, reaching $3\frac{1}{2}$ knots on a spring ebb. Further offshore, S of Scarweather and Nash Sands, rates are even stronger: up to 5 knots at springs on both flood and ebb. Unpredictable eddies occur near the shoals, and there are heavy overfalls off the W tail of Nash Sand on a weather-going tide.

Description

Swansea, or 'Abertawe' in the native Welsh, is a large provincial city which has grown up at the head of Swansea Bay where the River Tawe ends its journey through a long valley of mining villages. The Gower Peninsula forms the W shore of the bay, terminating in Mumbles Head with its distinctive pier and lifeboat slip. On the E side of the bay, the straight coastline between Porthcawl and Neath starts off in the S as sand-dunes and burrows, giving way at Port Talbot to a rather dour esplanade of smelting works, steel-rolling mills and factory chimneys.

The entrance to Swansea harbour is actually the mouth of the Tawe, where two long breakwaters reach out into deep water across the broad mudflats that fringe the bay. The tidal lock for the Swansea Yacht Haven is on the W bank of the river about ½ mile up from the pierheads. This marina is part of a recent ambitious development of the city's old maritime quarter; it is the best place for visitors to berth and has all possible facilities.

Swansea is straightforward of access and a good port of refuge. Even in heavy weather from the S or SW it is always possible to negotiate the breakwaters and reach shelter, although the sea can be very steep in Swansea Bay under these conditions. The dredged channel guarantees 3m LAT as far as the commercial dock entrance, just inside the harbour to starboard. Above this point the Tawe is fairly shallow and deeper draft yachts need about an hour's rise of tide above LWS to reach the marina lock.

Outer approaches

The approach along the coast from the W has been covered in the previous section on the Gower Peninsula. Once past the Mixon bell-buoy and clear to the E of Mumbles Head, set a course for the 'Swigg' (SW Inner Green

Swansea Yacht Haven is an attractive port of call for visitors and has excellent facilities. The marina is part of an ambitious development of the city's old maritime quarter. Access is by way of a tidal lock situated about ½ mile upstream from Swansea pierheads.

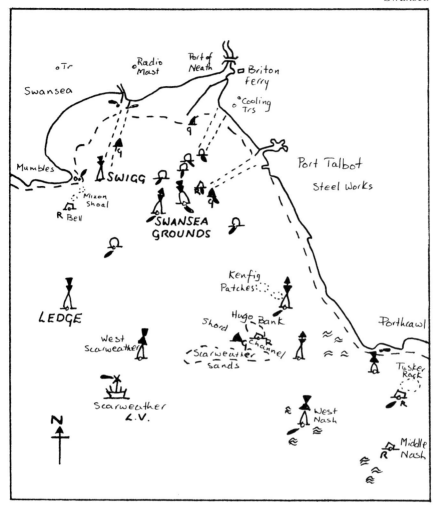

Approaches to Swansea Bay and Porthcawl

Grounds) S-cardinal buoy which lies just under a mile E by N of Mumbles lighthouse.

From the SE, the approach to Swansea involves keeping clear of Nash Sand and Scarweather Sands, and giving a good berth to the overfalls off Nash Point and in the region of the West Nash and Middle Nash buoys. If you are coming along the coast from Barry, the simplest tactic is to stay 1–1½ miles off Nash Point and to continue broadly W by N until you are about 2 miles S of West Nash W-cardinal buoy. Then make good to the NW, leaving the Scarweather lightvessel ½ mile to port and West Scarweather W-cardinal buoy close to starboard; beware of being set towards the sands if the tide is flooding. Swansea pierheads lie 8 miles due N true from the West Scarweather buoy.

In quiet weather, good visibility, and if the tide permits, it is possible to save some distance by cutting inside either Nash Sand or Scarweather Sands or both. By passing close under Nash Point you can take the Nash Passage between the headland and the East Nash E-cardinal buoy. This pass is less than $\frac{1}{4}$ mile wide and is best entered above half-tide, quite feasible if you leave Barry just before local HW with a view to carrying the full 6 hr of the Channel ebb westwards.

Once into the Nash Passage, make good about 307° Mag. so as to leave Tusker Rock red can buoy a cable to starboard and Porthcawl Point just under a mile to starboard, passing outside its overfalls. Now follow the coast a mile offshore, entering Swansea Bay by passing a cable E of Kenfig E-cardinal buoy. Once you are clear to the N of Kenfig Patches, make good 318° Mag. for the 8 miles to Swansea entrance green conical buoy.

Admiralty charts 1161 and 1169 are recommended for this shortcut, but in brisk weather or poor visibility it is prudent to use the big-ship route outside all the dangers.

Entry

Leave the Swigg S-cardinal bell buoy close either side and then make good 027° Mag. for $1\frac{1}{2}$ miles to the start of the dredged channel; this is marked on the E by green conical buoys.

The pontoon berths at Swansea Yacht Haven shown here before flats were built in the background. Opened in 1983, this was the Bristol Channel's first coastal marina, and it soon established a reputation for friendly service.

The signal lights are mounted inside the breakwaters on the E side of the river, at the pierhead just N of the main commercial lock. From seaward you will see 9 signal lights in 3 columns of 3. The centre light in the W column controls pleasure craft; when it is red, yachts should wait out in the holding area to the SW of the West Pier. Enter on a green light.

Having said all this, there are occasions when the signal lights seem to have been forgotten and left on 'stop'! If you suspect this may have happened, check with Port Control on VHF if you have it, or else proceed **with caution** against the signal until you are quite sure that the way is clear. The speed limit within the harbour is 5 knots.

Entry at night

Approaching from the W, the Mumbles light (Fl4W, 10s) is a key mark for providing clearing lines off the Gower coast. When coming up-Channel, a sound plan is to maintain an easterly track from the Helwick LtV towards the Ledge S-cardinal buoy moored 4 miles due S of the Mumbles. This line keeps you nicely outside Helwick Sands and clear of the Oxwich Point overfalls, although you can begin to borrow inshore once Mumbles light bears less than 050°Mag.

The Swigg bears 023°Mag. from the Ledge buoy, distant 4½ miles, and you usually need to allow for a good cross-tide. Check the set and drift carefully as you approach the Mumbles, and keep Oystermouth Castle (floodlit at night) open of Mumbles pierhead lights (2FR, vert) to clear the Cherry Stones race. The harbour leading lights in line 028°Mag. mark the E limit of the dredged channel and are obscured when bearing less than 028°Mag.; the front lights are two fixed vertical greens with a 2 mile range and the rear light is a single fixed green with a 6 mile range. The starboard hand channel buoys are lit (QG and FlG, 2.5s).

Approaching from the SE, strangers should stay outside Nash and Scarweather Sands and make for the Scarweather LtV (Fl5s). From here, head NNW for the Ledge buoy until you have passed W of the West Scarweather buoy (unlit), and then make good about 010°Mag., for the Swigg. Allow for the last of the W-going ebb if you have carried the tide down from Barry.

The Nash Passage is navigable at night with local knowledge, fair weather and good visibility. The trick is to make use of the NW sectors of Nash Point lighthouse (Fl2, RW, 10s), having first cut between the headland and the East Nash buoy (VQ3, 5s). The boundary between the red and white NW sectors leads along the inner track of 307°Mag. described earlier.

Berths and anchorages

Swansea Yacht Haven The marina has about 400 pontoon berths and there is always plenty of room for visitors. The lock into the wet basins is operated as the tide serves (approximately 3 hr either side of HW) between 0800 and 2200 during the season and 0800 and 1700 out of season. Details of lock-in and lock-out times are posted daily at marina reception, or they are available by radio on VHF Ch 37(M). Locking out of hours can be arranged with 24 hr notice or in emergencies, subject to tide.

Yachts arriving early may wait alongside just outside the gates. When the lock starts working there will be a metre of water over the outer sill. Visitors are allocated a berth as they lock through. The outer and inner basins are connected by a short channel, crossed by a swing bridge which is opened on demand.

Swansea Yacht Haven's extensive facilities include fresh water at the berths, diesel (but not petrol) alongside, contractors for hull and engine repairs, a Travel-lift, chandlery, chart agent, sailmaker, and electronic repairs and servicing. The marina is pleasantly situated S of the city centre, and it is only about 10 minutes' walk to a shopping precinct and a selection of Swansea's restaurants. Basic provisions, snacks and hot meals are available on-site at the Marina Cafe.

The River Tawe The Yacht Haven has four holding buoys about 100m downstream from the lock on the W side of the river, available for berth-holders and visitors when the lock is closed. Yachts should secure fore and aft; the LW depth is about 4ft and the bottom is soft mud.

It is sometimes possible to use one of the local moorings in the Tawe River, just below or just above the lock entrance on the E side of the river. Most of these dry out to soft mud at LWS, although yachts of moderate draft will just stay afloat at neaps.

Yachts preparing to lock out of Swansea Yacht Haven. The marina has over 400 pontoon berths and there is always plenty of room for visitors. The lock is operated as the tide serves between 0800 and 2200 during the season, and the marina is accessible for a good 3 hours either side of HW.

Briton Ferry

Summary Briton Ferry and the industrial Port of Neath lie at the mouth of the Neath River, which flows into Swansea Bay 3 miles ENE of Swansea entrance. The approaches are shallow and the river dries to thick mud, but entry is possible above half-tide. A 1½ mile buoyed channel follows a training wall marked by beacons. Strangers should only enter in daylight and moderate offshore weather. Inside the river on the W bank, Monkstone Cruising and Sailing Club have their own dredged yacht basin, just below the road bridge. The basin is sheltered and visitors are welcome.

Tides As for Swansea, i.e. at HW Milford Haven or HW Dover − 4 hr 50min. Heights above chart datum: 9.6m MHWS, 1.0m MLWS, 7.3m MHWN, 3.2m MLWN.

Port Control Neath Harbour Commissioners, tel Briton Ferry (0639) 2256. No VHF listening watch.

Tidal streams and currents

The streams in Swansea Bay are weak, but rates are faster in the offing. Refer to Swansea section for details. In the Neath River a spring ebb can reach 3 knots and a spring flood 2 knots, the rate and height being partly affected by the volume of fresh water coming down from inland.

Description

The Neath River wends its way seawards from the Fawr Forest through another South Wales mining valley, the Vale of Neath. Past Briton Ferry and the Port of Neath, the river emerges into Swansea Bay about 3 miles ENE of Swansea harbour entrance. The Neath estuary is shallow, drying at LW to a thick, unsavoury looking mud. The surrounding area is mostly industrial, with a scrap metal works sprawling on the E bank and Port Talbot not far away. Noise from the works' power hammers and the nearby M4 tends to work against a peaceful riverside atmosphere.

But over on the W bank, just below the road bridge, the friendly Monkstone Cruising and Sailing Club thrives amidst all this bustle. They have a well established clubhouse and their own yacht basin, which was excavated by the members in 1984 and now provides a sheltered haven with a least depth of about 1m.

The river is entered across mudflats by way of a 1½ mile buoyed channel, only accessible above half-tide. The channel is kept reasonably clear by a training wall on its SE side. Entry is fairly straightforward, the outer buoys lying about 3 miles N by E from Swansea Grounds E-cardinal buoy and a similar distance NE from the Swigg S-cardinal buoy. The Neath River is not a safe port of refuge—yachts should make for Swansea in heavy weather—but there is good shelter inside the yacht basin. The small town of Briton Ferry is 15 minutes' walk across the road bridge, but the Ferryboat Inn is handy on the W bank.

Outer approaches

As for Swansea, but make for Swansea Grounds E-cardinal buoy rather than the Swigg. Swansea Grounds lies 5 miles N by E from the West Scarweather W-cardinal buoy and 3 miles ESE from Mumbles Head. Then make good about 020°Mag. for 3 miles to come up with the outer marks of the Neath River entrance channel. Several cooling towers and chimneys are conspicuous on the E side of the estuary.

The Neath River flows into Swansea Bay 3 miles ENE of Swansea entrance. The approaches are shallow and the river dries to thick mud, but entry is possible above half-tide. Monkstone Cruising and Sailing Club have their own dredged yacht basin, just below the road bridge on the W bank.

Entry

The entrance channel lies between a slag training bank to port, marked by a number of red cans, and a 1½ mile training wall to starboard, marked by three well-spaced posts. A green conical outfall buoy about ¼ mile SE of the outer post serves as a kind of fairway buoy. Leave it well to starboard when entering and then make for the outer post.

Follow the channel to the NE, turning slightly to starboard when you reach the inner end of the training wall. Leave to starboard the rough slag breakwater that extends from the S pierhead of the disused Briton Ferry dock and follow the line of the E shore as the channel curves northwards. You will see the road bridge ahead and the club premises and basin on the W bank. Edge into the basin and ask one of the members about a berth.

The channel carries about 23ft of water at MHWS and 12ft at MHWN. Onshore winds from S and SW can make entry difficult.

Entry at night

It is not recommended that strangers enter the Neath River at night. However, the starboard hand posts on the training wall are lit as follows:
—The outer post, the Monkstone Light, exhibits two all-round greens.
—The middle post, about 1000m NE of Monkstone, exhibits one all-round green.
—The inner post, situated a short way seaward of the end of the slag breakwater, exhibits three all-round greens.
No great reliance should be placed on these lights as they are only inspected occasionally.

Port Talbot

Summary Port Talbot is just over 2 miles SE of the entrance to the Neath River, on the NE side of Swansea Bay. Its principal harbour is the huge iron ore terminal sheltered behind two large breakwaters and prohibited to yachts. But close to the N of this complex is the narrow estuary of the River Afan. The river doesn't quite dry, but is shallow at low springs and the bar at the entrance often breaks. You can normally enter 2 hr after LW, but avoid the Afan in fresh onshore winds. The Port Talbot Small Boat Club can usually arrange a mooring for visitors.

Tides HW Port Talbot is at HW Milford Haven −00hr 05min, or HW Dover −4hr 55min. Heights above chart datum: 9.6m MHWS, 1.0m MLWS, 7.3m MHWN, 3.3m MLWN.

Port Control None for the River Afan.

Tidal streams and currents

Rates in the NE corner of Swansea Bay are weak. In the River Afan itself a spring ebb can reach 3 knots and the flood $1\frac{1}{2}$ knots. Some 5 miles S of Port Talbot entrance, up to 4 knots can be experienced at springs in the vicinity of Kenfig Patches and Hugo Bank.

Description

The iron ore terminal at Port Talbot is an imposing sight from seaward. Steel mills and cooling towers dominate the skyline and the harbour's S breakwater is about a mile long. However, yachts are not allowed into this complex and must use the narrow estuary of the River Afan, close to the N. Entry to the Afan is straightforward from a pilotage point of view, but sufficient rise of tide is required over the bar, and over a wreck in the approaches. You can only get $\frac{1}{2}$ mile up the river, as far as the road bridge. Port Talbot Small Boat Club have some moorings below the bridge where you can stay afloat at neaps. The clubhouse and landing slip are on the S bank, above the disused entrance to the old docks. There are shops about 15 minutes' walk from the slip.

Outer approaches

As for Swansea and Briton Ferry, but the entrance to the Afan lies $3\frac{1}{2}$ miles NE of Swansea Grounds E-cardinal buoy. Approaching from the SSE along the coast, say from Porthcawl, pass a mile off Sker Point and just to the E of Kenfig E-cardinal buoy. Then make good about 325°Mag. for 5 miles, to come up with the outer pair of lateral buoys for the dredged channel into Port Talbot terminal.

Entry

Follow the line of the terminal entrance channel, but keep just to the N outside the fairway, leaving the two red can buoys and the N breakwater to starboard. Follow the breakwater round to the E to enter the Afan, leaving the old S pier well to port.

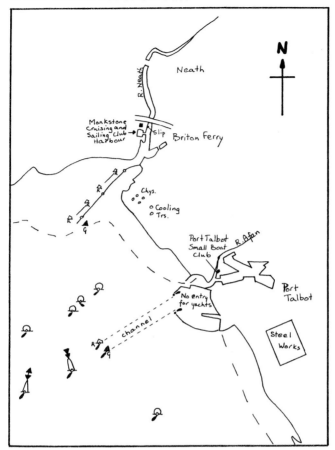

*Briton Ferry and
the River Neath*

Do not approach the Afan any earlier than 2 hr after LW, partly because of
the bar but also to be sure of clearing the wreck (dries 0.1m LAT) which lies
about ½ mile W by S from the end of the N breakwater. In moderate onshore
winds the bar will break until well after half-flood. Do not enter the river in
fresh onshore winds without local knowledge.

Entry at night

Reasonably straightforward in quiet weather. A pair of leading lights bring
you in from Swansea Bay towards the terminal entrance, leading close S of
Swansea Grounds E-cardinal and Cabenda S-cardinal buoys: front light
(OcR, 4s, 6M), rear light (OcR, 6s, 6M) in line bearing 068°Mag. The two red
can entrance buoys are lit: No. 1 (FlR, 5s) and No. 3 (FlR, 3s). The N
breakwater head is also lit (Fl4R, 10s), but the old S pier at the mouth of the
Afan is unlit.

Berths and anchorages

It is preferable to obtain the use of one of the Port Talbot Small Boat Club
moorings. Otherwise anchor in the river clear of the moorings, opposite the
disused entrance to the old docks.

Porthcawl

Summary Porthcawl, a seaside resort about 12 miles SE of Swansea entrance, has a small picturesque harbour enclosed by stone piers. The harbour dries to soft mud below half-tide and is well protected from the N and W, but winds from between E and S send in a nasty surge. The approach is from the SW, between Porthcawl Point and Fairy Rock W-cardinal buoy, before rounding the W breakwater and turning NW towards the entrance. Seaward of the breakwater, the tide flows strongly along the coast reaching 6 knots at springs.

Tides HW Porthcawl is at HW Milford Haven, or HW Dover −05hr 00min. Heights above chart datum are 9.9m MHWS, 1.0m MLWS, 7.5m MHWN, 3.3m MLWN.

Port Control Ogwr Borough Council. HM Mr Harry Grant, tel Porthcawl (065 671) 2756, summer months only.

Tidal streams and currents

Seaward of the W breakwater streams are strong, setting along the coast roughly WNW on the ebb and ESE on the flood. Spring rates sometimes reach 6 knots and the approaches can be rough in a weather-going tide. There is often turbulence off the breakwater, especially during the ebb, and heavy overfalls may occur up to $1\frac{1}{2}$ miles W of Porthcawl Point. Avoid being set towards Tusker Rock, an extensive drying reef $1\frac{1}{4}$ miles SE of Porthcawl entrance.

Description

In the middle part of the last century Porthcawl was a busy little coal port, although how even the handiest barges managed to work into the entrance under sail is a mystery to me. Under pressure of competition from Barry and Port Talbot, Porthcawl docks ceased trading in 1906 and the present small harbour, once the outer basin, is all that remains of a much larger complex. The inner basin was filled in after the last war to make a car park. No longer a port as such, Porthcawl remains a busy holiday resort for the Welsh Valleys.

The harbour is close to the town centre, which has a good selection of shops, restaurants and pubs. About 40 local boats are based at Porthcawl during the season, and moorings are occasionally available for visitors though yachts normally dry out against the E wall, next to one of the ladders. Make your number with the Harbour Master, whose office is on the W quay.

Strangers should only make for Porthcawl in quiet weather, since the approaches soon become rough in a weather-going tide. The harbour has a narrow dog's-leg entrance and offers good shelter in northerlies and westerlies, but even moderate winds from between E and S will send in an unpleasant swell. It has recently been proposed that the harbour be turned into a marina, which would be good news for visitors if not for the locals.

Outer approaches

Allow for the strong tidal streams when approaching Porthcawl. The entrance

Porthcawl harbour is a tiny place. You can see the old collapsed E breakwater just outside the entrance, and the post beacon is left close to starboard on the way in.

lies not quite 4 miles E of Scarweather Sands and only 1¼ miles NW of Tusker Rock, a notorious and extensive reef which dries to 4.2m. Tusker Rock uncovers as the harbour dries.

Coming from Swansea Bay, the most direct route lies between Sker Point and Kenfig Patches E-cardinal buoy, thence keeping a good mile off the coast to avoid the worst of the Porthcawl Point overfalls. When Porthcawl W breakwater head is bearing about ENE, steer so as to leave Fairy W-cardinal buoy ¼ mile to the S.

Coming from the E in moderate weather you may, if wind and tide are together, approach Porthcawl by cutting inside Nash Sand (see Swansea section for details of the Nash Passage). Stay S of Tusker Rock red can buoy and leave Fairy W-cardinal to the E. Coming from seaward, or from the E if conditions are unsuitable for the Nash Passage, leave West Nash W-cardinal buoy a good mile to the E and SE to avoid the overfalls off the end of Nash Sand. Then make to the ENE for Porthcawl.

Above half-tide, in quiet weather only, the locals cut straight across Nash Sand W of Middle Nash red can buoy. This can save you up to 7 miles when coming from the E, but take the deep-water passage round the West Nash buoy if in doubt about conditions.

Entry

Approach Porthcawl from the SW, leaving Fairy W-cardinal buoy 2 cables to starboard. There are drying rocky ledges close W of the W breakwater, so only head up for it when the lighthouse bears roughly N by W, distant 2 cables. Leave the breakwater head close to port, following its line hard along to the NW for a short way and then turing N off the wide landing slip to leave the beacon at the end of the old collapsed E breakwater to starboard. Enter the harbour an hour either side of HW.

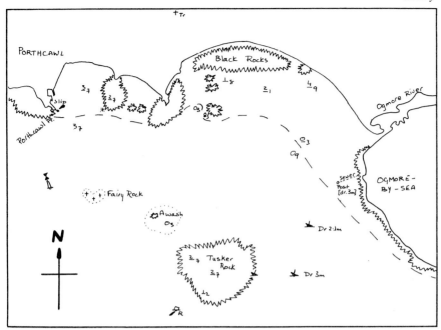

Approaches to Porthcawl

Entry at night

Not recommended for strangers, because of the strong tides off the entrance and the various dangers in the approaches. However, entry is possible using the sector light exhibited from the W breakwater head (FWRG), which leads in between 044°Mag. and 090°Mag. When you are a mile from the entrance stay on the green limit of the white sector, which leaves Fairy W-cardinal buoy (unlit) not quite 2 cables to starboard and clears the rocky ledges to the W of the W breakwater.

Berths and anchorages

If you are too early on the tide to enter the harbour there is a temporary anchorage about 3 cables SSE of Porthcawl W breakwater, but the holding is poor and the current strong. When berthing inside the harbour go alongside the E wall and ask the Harbour Master about the possibility of using a vacant mooring; otherwise dry out alongside the E wall next to one of the ladders.

Barry

Summary Barry harbour is easy of access by day or night and makes a useful refuge between Swansea and Penarth marinas. Barry Yacht Club have moorings in the W part of the outer harbour and yachts may lock into No. 1 dock by arrangement. The harbour lies just E of Barry Island and $3\frac{1}{2}$ miles WSW of Lavernock Point—keep clear of pilot launches and shipping when entering. There is a least depth of about 4m as far as the dock gates and pilot station, although the water soon shoals as you leave the entrance, and head towards the YC. Anchor just W of the fairway if arriving near LW, but tuck in nearer the club as soon as there is sufficient rise.

Tides HW Barry is at HW Avonmouth – 00hr 20min, or HW Dover – 04hr 35min. Heights above chart datum: 11.4m MHWS, 0.9m MLWS, 8.7m MHWN, 3.7m MLWN.

Port Control Associated British Ports. Barry Docks Radio on VHF Ch 16 (wkg Ch 10, 11, 22) from 4 hr before to 4 hr after HW. Dock Master tel Barry (0446) 732311.

Tidal streams and currents

The tides in the offing are strong, particularly W of Barry between Nash and Rhoose Points; spring rates here reach 5 knots and the streams more or less follow the line of the coast. There is a W-going set across the harbour entrance at all states of tide.

Description

Barry began life as a coal port, but the docks now handle a great variety of cargo. The town and environs are not picturesque but the outer harbour can be useful for yachts on passage, being accessible at all states of tide and under most conditions. The docks are steadily busy and Barry is also the headquarters of the Bristol Channel Pilots, so Barry Roads is a focus for shipping movements: keep this in mind when approaching and entering the harbour. Barry Yacht Club have their waterside premises next to the lifeboat slip in the W corner of the outer harbour. There is little spare space, but the BYC are always ready to help visiting yachtsmen and it is usually possible to use a vacant mooring.

Barry Island, now a peninsula, lies close to the W of the harbour and was once the haunt of pirates and smugglers. Its present trade is more prosaic, since most of the 'Island' is occupied by a holiday camp of intimidating proportions. Luckily, most of its inmates stay within the camp confines and

Looking northwestwards into Barry harbour from the entrance. The ship is entering the commercial docks, but the yacht moorings lie to the SW and W of the pilot station.

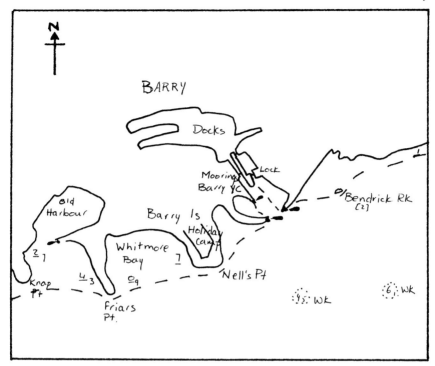

Barry Harbour

the harbour area is usually fairly quiet. Barry town is some way from the outer harbour, but there are several shops a short walk from the yacht club and a boatyard and chandlery right next door.

By arrangement with the Dock Master, yachts may enter No. 1 Dock via Lady Windsor Lock (contact Barry Docks Radio). This is recommended in strong winds from S and SE, when a nasty swell invades the outer harbour. Barry Old Harbour, just W of Barry Island, is now rarely used; it dries and is steadily silting up.

Outer approaches

Coming from the W, keep at least 6 cables off Breaksea Point, i.e. outside Breaksea power station intake structure (FlR) and its red can bell-buoy. Give a similar berth to Rhoose Point and the rocky shallows in the bay just beyond. You will notice traffic in and out of Cardiff Airport, which lies a little way back from the cliffs just W of Rhoose Point, and this stretch of coast also has several prominent tall chimneys.

Knap Point and Friars Point are fairly steep-to and between them is the entrance of Barry Old Harbour. You then pass Whitmore Bay and the large holiday camp (very conspic.) on Nell's Point, the SE corner of Barry Island. Barry harbour breakwaters will now be seen ½ mile to the NE. When making this passage from the W, remember that all headlands between Porthcawl and Barry have strong tidal streams flowing round them.

Coming from the E along the coast, say from Penarth, keep outside the Ranie buoy (unlit), ½ mile ESE of Lavernock Point. In fresh wind over tide

Barry harbour entrance looking south, with Steep Holm island in the distance. When approaching Barry, watch out for ships manoeuvring to pick up and drop off pilots.

conditions, then work offshore to the SSW so as to clear the broken water over Lavernock Spit (2.7m), which extends for over a mile S of Lavernock Point. If coasting close inshore in quiet weather do not cut inside Sully Island, which lies a mile or so WSW of Lavernock Point and is joined to the mainland by a half-tide causeway. When approaching Barry from the E, stay seaward of Bendrick Rocks which are about 400m ENE of the harbour entrance and never cover.

Approaching Barry from the S, there are no navigational dangers for yachts once Culver Sand (dries 4m) has been safely cleared. This long narrow bank lies about $6\frac{1}{2}$ miles due S of Barry harbour entrance, is nearly 4 miles from end to end and is guarded at its E and W extremities by cardinal buoys. The Breaksea LANBY is a prominent mark, moored just over 4 miles SW of the harbour entrance, but remember that ships converge on this buoy to pick up and drop off pilots.

Useful in poor visibility are the marine radiobeacon on Flat Holm island (296.5 kHz, **FL**, 50M, No. 4) and the aero radiobeacon close NE of Rhoose Point (363.5 kHz, **CDF**, 20M, cont.). The Breaksea LANBY is fitted with a Racon beacon.

Entry

Completely straightforward, between the E and W breakwaters in a NW direction, but note that the tidal set across the entrance is invariably W-going. Once inside the pierheads you will see a short, dividing mole ahead and slightly to port. Just to the E of this mole is the Lady Windsor Lock which leads through to Barry Docks. To the W is a shallow bay with local moorings and Barry YC at its head. The bay dries at LAT to thick mud, but much of it has a couple of feet of water at ordinary LWS. Close N of the club is a lifeboat slip, its end marked by a beacon. The pilot station is on the W side of the dividing mole; do not obstruct access to the pilot's quay.

Entry at night

As for daytime, but note that the coast is unlit between Nash Point lighthouse

The outer harbour at Barry, which dries about 2 hours either side of LW. Barry is easy of access by day or night and makes a useful refuge between Swansea and Penarth marinas.

(Fl2, WR, 10s) and Barry harbour. The St Hilary radio mast 4½ miles inland from Breaksea Point shows a quick flashing red aero light and 4 fixed vertical reds. There is a light-tower on Barry W breakwater head (FlW, 2.5s) and a structure on the E breakwater head (QG). Also 2 fixed vertical red lights are shown from the end of the pilots' pier when vessels are prohibited from entering or leaving the harbour. Flat Holm island (Fl3, WR, 10s) and Breaksea LANBY (Fl 15s) are both useful lights when approaching Barry at night.

Berths and anchorages

Outer Harbour You can anchor close N of the W breakwater in thick mud, staying afloat at neaps and touching the bottom at low springs. Keep clear of the pilots' fairway. Contact Barry YC for the possible use of one of their members' moorings, but the berths nearest the clubhouse dry out. There is basic shopping just up the hill behind the harbour, water is available at the club, but fuel involves a long walk into town.

No. 1 Dock Yachts can pass through the Lady Windsor Lock by arrangement with the Dock Master, a wise move if strong winds are expected from the S or SE.

Penarth Port Marina

Summary Penarth Port Marina, run by Camper & Nicholson, is the latest yacht haven on the South Wales coast. Converted from the old Penarth coal dock, it now provides a strategically placed cruising base and passage port for the E Bristol Channel. Penarth itself is a pleasant seaside town, tucked behind Lavernock Point just S of Cardiff. The marina is close S of the mouth of the River Ely and is entered via a buoyed channel and a sea lock. The approaches are straightforward and the lock is accessible for about 9 hr in 12 at neaps, and 7½ hr at springs. The marina has all the usual facilities.

Tides HW Penarth is at HW Avonmouth −00hr 15min, or HW Dover −04hr 30min. Heights above chart datum outside Penarth Lock: 12.2m MHWS, 0.9m MLWS, 9.4m MHWN, 3.6m MLWN. The outer lock sill is 3.5m above chart datum.

Port Control Camper & Nicholsons (Marina) Ltd. The Berthing Master listens on VHF Ch 16 and 37(M) between 0800 and 2200 during the season.

Tidal streams and currents

Streams in the marina approaches are moderate, reaching 2 knots at springs off the entrance and in Cardiff Roads. Further out, near Monkstone lighthouse, rates reach 4 knots at springs. Off Lavernock Point, a spring ebb can run up to 5 knots for the middle 2 hr.

Description

The seaside town of Penarth occupies a pleasant position on the W side of the Taff and Ely estuary, a mile or two S of Cardiff. Penarth's attractive sea-front faces up the Severn and is sheltered from the prevailing westerlies. The beach and pier are popular during the season, but the tourism is never frantic. Penarth Yacht Club have their elegant premises at the S end of the Esplanade, and ships pass close by on their way to and from Cardiff Docks.

Penarth Dock, just N of the town, started life as a coal port in 1865. It has been virtually disused since the last war, but Camper & Nicholson have now converted the outer basin into a marina which will soon expand into the much larger inner basin. Entry is by way of a sea lock which, for a boat drawing 1½m, is accessible for about 4½ hr either side of HW at neaps and about 3¾ hr either side of HW at mean springs. There is a waiting jetty outside the lock, accessible about an hour before the lock can open. A buoyed channel 200m long and 15m wide connects with the main shipping fairway between Cardiff Docks and the sea. The entrance is sheltered from the W, but somewhat exposed to winds from between ENE and SSE.

Penarth Port has all the usual marina facilities, and the surrounding area will eventually be developed and landscaped. Diesel and water are available alongside and there is good shopping nearby at Penarth.

Cardiff skyline from seaward.

Outer approaches

Penarth approaches are fairly straightforward, Cardiff Grounds bank being the main danger in the offing. Coming from the S or W, clear Lavernock Point by ¾ mile and pass between Ranie port-hand buoy and South Cardiff S-cardinal bell buoy. Then make good due N Mag. for 2 miles, leaving the Outer Wrach W-cardinal buoy close to starboard and Penarth Pier a good 2 cables to port. You now enter the shipping fairway (dredged to 1.2m), keeping a red can to port to clear the rocky ledges off Penarth Head. The channel leads NNE towards Cardiff Docks, with green conicals to starboard. To port, a line of smaller buoys marks the marina entrance channel.

Coming from the E via Bristol Deep, stay well S of Monkstone lighthouse and continue WSW for 1¾ miles to leave South Cardiff S-cardinal buoy close to the N. Then head N Mag. and proceed as above. Approaching Penarth from the NE, say from Newport or the River Rhymney, you will usually pass between Cardiff Grounds and Cardiff Flats, turning into the Taff estuary at the Outer Wrach.

The dredged fairway from the Outer Wrach buoy is negotiable under virtually all conditions of wind and tide. Strong winds from the E make for a choppy approach to the marina lock, although Cardiff Grounds and Cardiff Flats serve as partial breakwaters from that quarter. In heavy easterly weather try to arrive at Penarth soon after half-flood; you'll have plenty of water in the marina entrance channel, but there will not be enough depth over the outer banks to erode their protection.

Entry

Having followed the shipping fairway into the Taff estuary from the Outer Wrach W-cardinal buoy, turn to port opposite the Inner Wrach green conical, along the narrower buoyed channel which leads to the marina lock. Make fast alongside the waiting jetty until the gates open fully and a green light signals you in. Secure fore and aft inside the lock, tending your warps as the level changes. The Berthing Master will give you directions.

Entry at night

Monkstone lighthouse (Fl, 5s) is a key mark in the approach from the E, and Flat Holm island (F13, WR, 10s) in the approach from the S and W. The red sectors of Flat Holm shine over Cardiff Grounds to the N, and over Wolves Rock (dries 1.8m) and the various shoals off Lavernock Point to the NW.

All buoys mentioned under 'outer approaches' are lit. Off Lavernock Point, which is unlit, it is important to pass between Ranie port lateral buoy (Fl2R, 5s) and South Cardiff S-cardinal (Q6+LFl, 15s). Then make directly for the Outer Wrach (Q9, 15s), picking up the fairway leading lights (a pair of fixed whites in line bearing 357° Mag.) which are situated on the Cardiff shore about a mile N of the marina entrance. The Inner Wrach buoy is lit (FlG, 2.5s), and the smaller marina entrance buoys have quick-flashing green and red lights.

Berths and anchorages

Apart from berthing in the marina, there are a few possibilities for anchoring elsewhere in the Taff and Ely estuary.

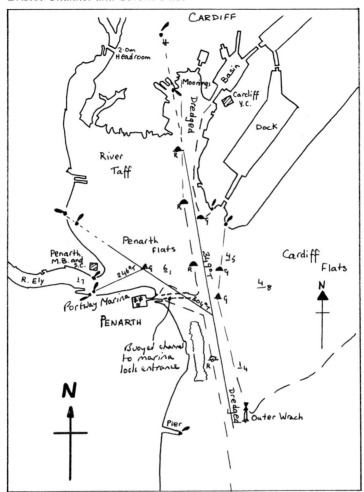

Portway Marina, River Ely, Cardiff and the approaches to the River Taff

The River Ely Near neaps, you can stay afloat in the mouth of the Ely, anchoring close SE of the Penarth Motor Boat and Sailing Club in about 2m LWN over mud. The club have an alongside pontoon a little way upstream on the N bank and they may also be able to let you use a vacant mooring further up the river. Both the pontoon and the moorings dry to thick mud. At night, two sets of fixed white leading lights (304°T and 246°T) lead into the River Ely from a position near the marina entrance. These can be useful if the marina lock is not operating and you want to make for the club anchorage.

Off Cardiff Yacht Club Cardiff YC have their premises on the E side of the Taff estuary near the city. Carry on up the shipping fairway past the entrance to Cardiff Docks, and then continue N for a further ½ mile. You will find some moorings, a few drying pontoon berths and limited room to anchor. Part of the harbour is dredged to 1.4m, but most dries to thick mud and has little to recommend it.

Local moorings in the River Ely, which dry below about half-tide. Portway Marina is in the background, on the S side of the river mouth.

Off Penarth Town In settled westerly weather you can anchor off Penarth itself, about ¼ mile SE of the Penarth YC landing slip, in 2m LAT over mud and sand. Make sure you are well inside the shipping fairway and show a riding light at night. This anchorage can be convenient if you are bound eastwards and want to leave Penarth just before LW. By berthing in the marina, you would lose at least 2 hr of flood tide before you were able to lock out.

Rhymney River

Summary The Rhymney River is a narrow tidal pill about 3½ miles NNE of the entrance to the Taff and Ely estuary. The approaches dry to over a mile offshore at LAT and strangers should only attempt entry near HW. There is a small local club a little way up the river. The immediate surroundings can seem rather bleak, close to the Cardiff Docks link road with a steel works not far away. But the river flows through wild marshland and has a curiously restful atmosphere. In quiet weather it makes an interesting call for small, shoal-draft boats and visitors are always welcome.

Tides HW in the Rhymney River is at HW Avonmouth −00h 15min, or HW Dover −04hr 30min. Approximate heights above datum: 12.1m MHWS, 0.6m MLWS, 9.2m MHWN, 3.3m MLWN.

Port Control None. The local moorings are administered by the Rhymney River Motor Boat, Sail and Angling Club: members sometimes listen on VHF Ch 16, or on their club's CB radio, Ch 40.

Tidal streams and currents

The streams in the immediate approaches can reach 2–3 knots at springs,

Local moorings in the Rhymney River. This narrow tidal pill lies about 3½ miles NE of Portway Marina. The approaches dry to over a mile offshore at LAT and strangers should only attempt entry near HW.

flowing more or less along the line of the coast and thus directly across the entrance channel.

Description

The Rhymney River is an unusual little backwater a few miles up the Severn Estuary from Cardiff and Penarth. Its narrow mouth faces SE and may be approached near HW by way of a winding channel across broad, off-lying mudflats. This channel is kept buoyed by the members of the Rhymney River Motor Boat, Sail and Angling Club, whose small clubhouse stands on the W bank of the river about ½ mile up from the entrance. The members' boats are generally under 25ft and shallow draft, and these should also be the main qualifications for any visiting craft.

The nearby steel works lend a rather gloomy aspect to the Rhymney, but in fact the river flows through wild, marshy scrubland and the club members' moorings represent a pocket haven of peace and quiet amidst the industrial outskirts of Cardiff. There are no shops nearby, but water is available at the clubhouse which has its own landing stage. The river dries to thick mud at about half-ebb. Although it is inadvisable to approach the Rhymney in fresh onshore winds, there is good shelter once you are inside and past the first bend.

Outer approaches

The North Cardiff green conical buoy marks the N extremity of the Cardiff Grounds banks; it lies about 2 miles SSE of the mouth of the Rhymney River and serves as a fairway buoy for the Rhymney entrance. Make for the North Cardiff whether you are coming from down-Channel, up-Channel or from across the Severn.

The tide is critical when entering the Rhymney; strangers should not arrive off the outer buoys until 1 hr before HW. Therefore it is unusual for anyone to approach the river directly from the E via Bristol Deep, as the flood will have been running strongly up-Channel for nearly 5 hr. Conversely, if you lock out of Penarth marina about 1½ hr before HW, you'll be well placed to take the last of the flood up towards the Rhymney. Do not attempt entry in fresh winds from between E and S.

Entry

From a position near the North Cardiff buoy steer about NW towards a conspicuous pumping station on the shore, some way down-Channel of the river entrance. The top of this building is mostly glass and often looks like a white band from seaward. You will soon pick up the first of the Rhymney club members' buoys, a small green can to be left close to starboard. 3 cables or so to port you will see a larger red can buoy which marks the end of a sewer outfall; this buoy has nothing directly to do with the Rhymney entrance channel, although it is a useful guide in the approach (there are a number of similar sewer buoys along this stretch of coast and you should not pass to landward of them). Continue to the NW past two more green cans, the second of which is paired with a red-and-white post. Now turn to the NE to follow the

Rhymney River (Chart by courtesy of the Rhymney River Motor Boat, Sail and Angling Club)

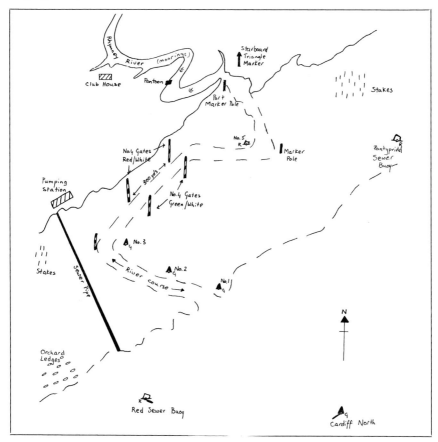

line of the shore, passing between two pairs of green-and-white and red-and-white posts; these are known locally as the No. 4 gates.

Now turn almost due E for a short way, leaving No. 5 red can buoy to port and another green-and-white post to starboard. The channel finally swings to the NNW and you now steer straight for the entrance; aim to leave a 'Dayglo' red triangular beacon on the E bank to starboard, before turning hard-a-port into the river.

On this last leg before reaching the mouth, avoid being set up-Channel to the NE: on this side of the entrance the bottom is foul with dangerous metal stakes. Once inside the river keep to the middle, following to starboard round the first bend and fetching up in the reach opposite the clubhouse.

Entry at night

On no account should strangers attempt to enter the Rhymney River at night. Although the North Cardiff buoy is lit (QG), the club buoys and post are all unlit and it is virtually impossible to pick up the entrance channel.

Berths and anchorages

You can anchor anywhere in the river providing you keep clear of local moorings, but the best stretch is just opposite the clubhouse. Because the river is narrow it is preferable either to anchor fore-and-aft, or to run out a kedge to make a standing moor. The Rhymney dries out to thick mud soon after half-ebb.

Newport and the River Usk

Summary The Usk flows into the Severn Estuary 9 miles NE of Cardiff Roads and 10 miles WNW of Avonmouth. The river mouth faces S and is fringed with mudflats, but a buoyed fairway leads as far as Newport Docks and there is plenty of water in the entrance above half-tide. Keep clear of ships using the fairway. Yachts are not allowed into the Docks, but Newport and Uskmouth SC have their clubhouse on the S bank of the river, $\frac{3}{4}$ mile up from the mouth. The area is heavily industrial and the Usk dries most of its width to dubious looking mud, but a narrow channel in mid-stream affords a reasonable anchorage off the club.

Tides HW Newport is at HW Avonmouth −00hr 15min, or HW Dover −04hr 30min. Heights above chart datum: 12.1m MHWS, 0.2m MLWS, 9.0m MHWN, 2.9m MLWN.

Port Control Newport Docks are run by Associated British Ports, but yachts are not subject to port control.

Tidal streams and currents

Spring streams offshore can reach 4–5 knots in Bristol Deep and 3–4 knots in Newport Deep, giving a tricky cross-set if you approach the Usk near half-tide. The streams in the river itself can also reach 4–5 knots at springs, particularly on the ebb. It is generally preferable to enter the Usk a little before HW slack.

Description

The Usk is a long river, starting its seaward journey in wild, mountainous country near the Brecon Beacons. Unfortunately for coastal boat owners, the last few miles through industrial Newport are the least attractive. At low tide, below the town bridges, all that remains of the Usk is a narrow, murky stream winding between factories and piles of mud. It is difficult to believe that, far up-river, fine salmon lurk in clear pools.

Nothing keeps boating people down, though, and the members of Newport and Uskmouth Sailing Club have, under adverse conditions, built their own premises on the S bank of the river. The outlook is rather bleak, with a power

Newport and the River Usk

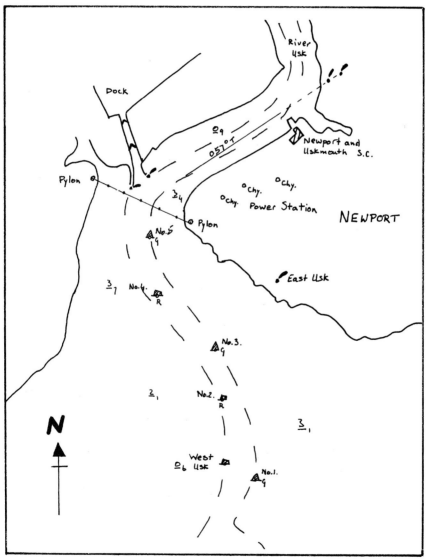

station just downstream and dock buildings opposite, and the local boats settle onto an unsavoury looking bed soon after half-ebb. But if, as a visitor, you anchor in the channel here, you will find good shelter, secure holding and a warm welcome at the club. Shops are not easily accessible, since the club lies within a fenced complex owned by Uskmouth Power Station, so it is wise to be self-sufficient in stores.

Outer approaches

The Usk entrance is fringed with mud. In the offing, to the S and E, are the extensive drying sandbanks known as the Usk Patch, Middle Grounds and Welsh Grounds, parts of which dry to nearly 10m. Local boats sail over these banks when the tide serves, especially when bound to and from the E, but strangers should stick to the channels except in quiet weather near HW.

Five miles S of the mouth of the Usk, the main Severn channel divides near the English and Welsh Grounds light-float; Bristol Deep leads upstream towards Avonmouth and Newport Deep turns NE towards the Welsh shore. Newport Deep green conical buoy, marking the SW extremity of Usk Patch bank, serves as the outer mark for the approach to the Usk. Below about half-tide, while the Middle and Welsh Grounds are uncovered, the powerful streams in Bristol Deep follow the line of the deepest water. Above half-tide the streams run broadly NE or SW, in the general direction of the Severn estuary, setting across the buoyed channel in places.

If approaching Newport from down-Channel, aim to make a position $\frac{1}{2}$ mile W of the English and Welsh Grounds light-float about $1\frac{1}{2}$ hr before HW Newport. From here make good about 022°Mag. for $2\frac{1}{2}$ miles to leave Newport Deep green conical buoy $\frac{1}{2}$ mile to starboard, and then make good 030°Mag. for a similar distance to the first pair of Newport entrance buoys, i.e. the West Usk red can bell-buoy and No. 1 green conical.

Coming from Penarth, lock out of the marina at half-flood. Stay inside Cardiff Grounds bank and leave the North Cardiff buoy close to starboard. Then follow the line of the shore to leave Newport Deep buoy $\frac{3}{4}$ mile to starboard before heading NNE for the Usk entrance. Coming down-Channel from Avonmouth, leave the pierheads about 2 hr before local HW and push the last of the flood to arrive off Newport at, or soon after, HW there.

Entry

Entry to the Usk is straightforward above half-tide, once the West Usk and No. 1 buoys have been located. Follow the buoyed fairway as far as the dock entrance and then turn to starboard up the river, keeping slightly to the S of centre. At MLWS there is a least depth of about 0.3m in the channel, so a good hour's rise of tide is necessary for even shallow draft boats. The tidal stream is perhaps a more critical factor than the depth, and entry near HW will ensure relatively still conditions for manoeuvring and anchoring. Fetch up opposite the Newport and Uskmouth Sailing Club, just beyond the power station and about 10m outside the local moorings.

Entry at night

Approach as by day, using the English and Welsh Grounds light-float (LFl, 10s) and Newport Deep bell buoy (Fl3G, 10s). If coming up-Channel leave both these lights $\frac{1}{2}$ mile to starboard; if coming down-Channel via Bristol

Deep, pass the light-float ½ mile to the N before turning northwards for Newport Deep. The East Usk light (Fl2, WRG) on the E side of the river mouth is the key mark in the entrance, its white sector leading W of Newport Deep buoy and up to the West Usk (QR) and No. 1 (QG) buoys. From here follow the lit buoys to the dock pierhead (2FR vert) and then pick up a pair of leading lights situated on the E shore of the river, just upstream from the sailing club beyond Julian's Pill. These are fixed green lights, to be kept in transit bearing 065°Mag. Think about anchoring after about ½ mile on this line.

Departure from Newport

If you are bound down the Bristol Channel from Newport, leave the River Usk about 2 hr before local HW so as to take full advantage of the next period of W-going tide. If you are bound up-Channel towards Avonmouth or the Upper Severn, leave the Usk as soon as you can after local LW.

Berths and anchorages

River Usk Anchor in the river opposite the club and about 10m outside the local moorings. It is preferable to moor to two anchors laid in line with the tide, and a riding light is necessary at night. Sometimes it is possible to use one of the moorings for a short stay, but enquire at the clubhouse first. Do not moor alongside the club pontoon, except briefly near HW to take on fresh water.

St Julian's Pill Just beyond the club, on the S side of the river, is a narrow creek called St Julian's Pill where you can anchor out of the tide and settle into soft mud near LW.

St Pierre Pill

Summary St Pierre Pill is a narrow drying inlet on the N shore of the Severn estuary, about 1½ mile below the Severn Bridge and ¾ mile N by E from Charston Rock lighthouse. Although open to the S, St Pierre is partly protected from that direction by the natural breakwaters of Charston Rock and Charston Sands; it provides a sheltered bolt-hole if, for example, you are bound upstream towards Sharpness and decide that you are too late on the tide. Several local boats are moored in the Pill during the season, mostly belonging to members of the Chepstow and District Yacht Club.

Tides HW St Pierre Pill is at HW Avonmouth +00hr 10min, or HW Dover −04hr 05min. Approximate heights above chart datum: 13.2m MHWS, 0.8m MLWS, 9.9m MHWN, 3.2m MLWN.

Port Control None. The local moorings are administered by the Chepstow and District Yacht Club, whose members sometimes listen on VHF Ch 16 and 37(M).

Tidal streams and currents

In this part of the Severn estuary streams can be fierce, sometimes reaching 8 knots at springs in the Shoots, $1\frac{1}{2}$–2 miles S by W of St Pierre Pill. Off the mouth of the Pill and in the vicinity of the Severn Bridge, spring rates can reach 5–6 knots.

Description

St Pierre Pill, a small drying inlet on the N shore of the Severn estuary, is in peaceful rural surroundings $1\frac{1}{2}$ miles below the Severn Bridge and a similar distance N by E from the Shoots channel. Charston Rock and Charston Sands lie $\frac{1}{2}$–$\frac{3}{4}$ mile to the S of the Pill, providing a natural breakwater which usually leaves a relatively quiet area of water off its mouth. The Pill is the base for members of the Chepstow and District Yacht Club, who maintain moorings there during the season.

St Pierre is a useful little haven in that rather forbidding stretch of the Severn between Avonmouth and Sharpness. It is worth considering if you are bound upstream for Sharpness and find yourself late on the tide, or if you are coming downstream and suspect, at the Severn Bridge, that conditions in the Shoots are likely to be nastier than you had bargained for. There is not much room in the Pill for visitors, but it is usually possible to squeeze in somewhere. Anchor fore-and-aft to prevent swinging, and buoy both anchors.

The clubhouse is built on the E arm of the Pill, above the low red cliffs that are prominent from the S. A narrow drying spit marked by withies extends SSW from these cliffs. There is a landing jetty off the W arm but no other facilities. The nearest shops are at Mathern village about a mile inland. Entry to the Pill is possible for 2 hr either side of HW, and the inlet dries to soft mud soon after half-ebb.

Outer approaches

Coming up-Channel, follow the directions for the Upper Severn (see pages 74ff), leaving Avonmouth $1\frac{1}{2}$ hr before HW there. Having passed the Upper Shoots beacon continue up the Shoots channel, but aim to leave Charston lighthouse about 300m to starboard: i.e. pass between the lighthouse and Black Rock Point. Then keep a similar distance off the shore, following round to the NNE towards St Pierre. Approach the mouth of the Pill from the SSW.

Coming down-Channel, pass under the Severn Bridge and leave Chapel Rock lighthouse about $\frac{1}{4}$ mile to starboard. Then make good 260°Mag. for $1\frac{1}{2}$ miles towards St Pierre, taking care to close the shore well before the mouth is reached so as to tuck inside Charston Sands. When about 2 cables from the bank follow its line to the SW until the mouth of the Pill bears more than N Mag. and then turn to starboard to approach the inlet from the SSW.

NB A sometimes alarming local phenomenon is that the tidal turbulence in the vicinity of the Shoots channel and Charston lighthouse is likely to cause false echo-sounder readings.

Entry

Enter within 2 hr of HW. The spit that extends from the E arm of the Pill is marked by withies and, sometimes, a small barrel buoy. Approach from the SSW, leaving the withies to starboard and the line of local moorings close to port. Sound carefully as you come into the inlet and fetch up wherever you can find room.

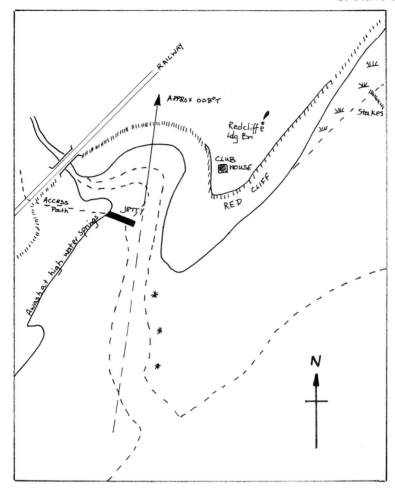

St Pierre Pill

Entry at night

Not advisable except in an emergency, but locals can edge into the Pill using the arcs of visibility of Redcliffe leading lights.

Berths and anchorages

In the Pill Anchor fore-and-aft and buoy both anchors. Sometimes it is possible to use a vacant mooring, but ask one of the locals first. Temporary berthing is allowed alongside the jetty on the W side of the inlet. The Pill dries out to soft mud soon after half-ebb.

Mathern Oaze Near neaps and in settled weather it is possible to anchor in the river NE of St Pierre, off the stretch of shore between the Pill and the mouth of the Wye known as Mathern Oaze. Edge as close in as the tide will allow; the bottom is mud.

The River Wye and Chepstow

The Wye joins the Severn estuary just W of Beachley Point, and the Severn Bridge crosses its mouth. Barges once used the quays at Chepstow, 2 miles upstream, but only small boats moor there now. Although mostly drying, the Wye provides one or two pools where keelboats can stay afloat at LW. Perhaps the most convenient for yachts on passage is just above the Severn Bridge. Moor bows to two anchors laid in line with the tide, opposite a red beacon on the W bank. While not exactly picturesque this spot makes a bolt-hole if you miss the Severn tide, whether you are bound upstream for Sharpness or downstream for the Shoots.

Lydney

Summary Lydney Dock lies on the N bank of the River Severn, about 8 miles above the Severn Bridge opposite Berkeley Power Station. Once used by barges and small coasters, the port is now virtually derelict commercially. Yet the lock still functions and yachts may enter the wet basin on weekdays near HW, by giving due notice to Sharpness Radio. Lydney YC have their premises on the N side of the lock; members' boats are moored in the basin and at drying river berths close N of the pierhead. There have been proposals to convert Lydney Dock into a marina, but its future remains uncertain.

Tides HW Lydney is at HW Avonmouth +00hr 35min, or HW Dover −03hr 40min. Approximate heights above chart datum: 9.4m MHWS, 0.4m MLWS, 6.1m MHWN, 0.1m MLWN. LW height in these upper reaches of the Severn is affected by fresh water flow, and may be raised by up to a metre.

Port Control Contact Sharpness Radio for entry to Lydney Dock (VHF Ch 16, working Ch 14).

Tidal streams and currents

The river ebb starts running soon after local HW and the flood soon after local LW. The strongest streams are in mid-river and on the Berkeley side, reaching 5 knots on a spring ebb. Rates are less fierce close off Lydney lock, especially on the flood.

Description

Lydney Dock, once a small but active coasting port serving the Forest of Dean, has gradually fallen into disuse despite several attempts to revive it for pleasure boating. However, it is still possible to pass through the lock into the wet basin, where some members of Lydney Yacht Club keep their boats. There is good shelter either in the main dock or in the old canal that leads up towards Lydney, and quite large yachts can be accommodated alongside the quays. Outside the lock, close N of the entrance pierhead, there are some drying berths along the river foreshore.

    Lydney is straightforward to approach, once you have made the tricky passage up the Severn estuary from Avonmouth. There is no obvious reason

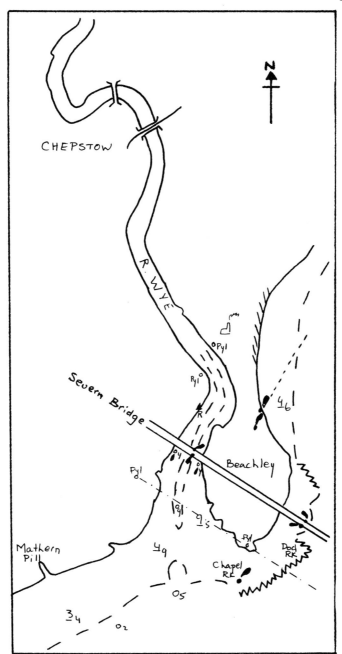

River Wye to Chepstow

for calling there when you are cruising, but the dock does provide a secure berth for laying-up, or if you have to leave a boat unattended. Before visiting Lydney it is a good idea to contact the yacht club (tel 0594-42573), just to check that the lock is still operating. There are no shops or other facilities near the dock and Lydney town is $1\frac{1}{2}$ miles inland.

The approach to Lydney from north-eastward. You can see the slip and some local drying berths, and the entrance to Lydney Dock is just behind the pierhead.

Outer approaches

Coming up-Channel, follow the directions for the Upper Severn (see pages 74ff). When abreast Berkeley Power Station turn to the NW, stemming the flood, and crab in a northerly direction over Saniger sands towards Lydney pier. If you are carried upstream past the pier, edge close to the W shore where the relatively slack water will enable you to motor back towards the lock.

Entry

At least 4 hr notice should be given to Sharpness Radio if you wish to enter Lydney Dock. The lock is only worked on weekdays, except by special arrangement, and entry is normally from 1 hr before until HW. The lock entrance is just S of the pier: watch out for the cross-set, even on the last of the flood.

Entry at night

There is no entry to Lydney Dock at night, except by special arrangement.

Berths and anchorages

In the Dock Moor alongside the quays in the dock itself, or further up the old canal towards Lydney. Silting is taking place in parts of the dock, so edge alongside the quays with care.

River berths Local boats dry out on legs about 100m upstream from Lydney pier; it is sometimes possible for visitors to find a vacant spot here, but you need to tuck right in out of the tide. The nearest safe anchorages are: 5½ miles downstream on the W side of the river, close inshore opposite a white house situated 3 cables due N of the Inward Rocks leading lights; also in Slime Road just above the Severn Bridge.

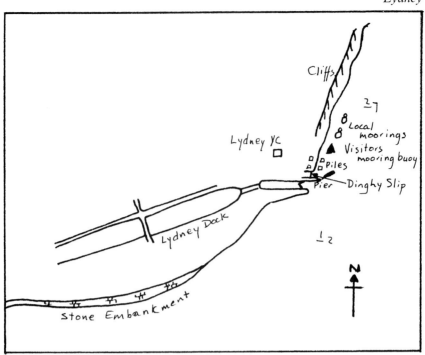

Lydney

The River Severn from Avonmouth to the bridge

The River Severn from the bridge to Sharpness

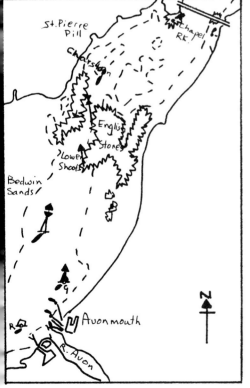

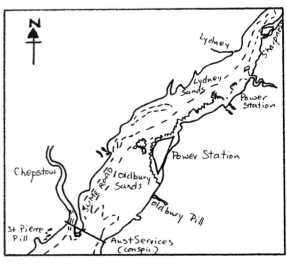

The peaceful local moorings just above the entrance to Lydney Dock, on the west side of the Severn opposite Sharpness.

The River Severn from Avonmouth to Sharpness

The 17 mile passage up the Severn from Avonmouth to Sharpness requires careful pilotage and sound seamanship. Undoubtedly fascinating in fine weather, this potentially treacherous stretch of water is not to be trifled with on account of the powerful tides, numerous shoals and the shallowness of the upper reaches. The channel is fairly well marked, but there are several tricky turns where the navigator has to keep his wits about him, especially in poor visibility. The passage can be taken at night, using the various sets of leading lights, but strangers should stick to clear daylight and gentle winds. Use Admiralty chart 1166 or Stanford chart 14, in conjunction with local tide tables if possible. A pilot can be taken if required, tel Dursley (0453) 811323.

The tide and passage timing are the key factors for safe navigation. The rise and fall at Avonmouth can exceed 13m at springs, and although neap rates in the river are around 2–3 knots, spring rates can touch 8–10 knots in places. It is important not to start out too early from Avonmouth or you can find yourself running out of water with the fast-flowing flood pushing you onward. Conversely, if you attempt the passage too late the ebb will have set in before you reach Sharpness. It is a good idea to inform Sharpness Radio in advance of your trip, giving date and time of departure, destination, ETA and particulars of your boat (Ch 16, working Ch 14). Confirm your departure with Avonmouth Radio (Ch 16, working Ch 12 and 14).

Yachts should aim to arrive off Sharpness about $\frac{1}{2}$ hr before HW there, i.e. just before HW Avonmouth. If you can motor at 5 or 6 knots the trip should only take about $1\frac{3}{4}$–2 hr in a good run of tide, so leave Avonmouth pierheads about 2 hr before HW there. Faster boats must leave correspondingly later and slower boats a little earlier. Keep clear of commerical shipping entering or leaving Avonmouth. From the entrance, make good 010°Mag. for just under 2 miles to leave the Bedwin E-cardinal buoy 2 cables to port. Reasonable visibility is particularly important on this first stretch since the marks are well spaced and the flood sets strongly across your track to the NE. Although yachts should always give way to ships using the buoyed channel, there is much to be said for holding well up-tide on the W side of the fairway, rather than risk slipping towards the dangers on the E side.

Three miles up from Avonmouth you enter The Shoots, a narrow channel between the rocky English Stones shoal to the E and various smaller drying patches to the W. Make good about 020° Mag. from the Bedwin buoy towards Charston lighthouse, a white tower with a black horizontal band built on a drying reef some $\frac{3}{4}$ miles NE of Sudbrook Point. Redcliffe leading lights are situated on the W side of the river, behind and in line with Charston. These two fixed blue fluorescent lights are on all the time. Keep carefully on this three-point transit, leaving the Lower Shoots beacon (green conical topmark) and the Upper Shoots beacon (W-cardinal topmark) each a good cable to starboard.

Once past the Upper Shoots beacon borrow to the W of the leading line and take a slight curve to port, until you are between $\frac{1}{4}$ and $\frac{1}{2}$ mile SSW of Charston lighthouse. The tide will still be setting athwart your course. Come round to the NE, leaving Charston $1\frac{1}{2}$ cables to port, and head for the middle of the

Approaching the Shoots Channel and the Severn Suspension Bridge on the tricky passage between Avonmouth and Sharpness. The Lower Shoots beacon is just coming up and should be left a good cable to starboard.

The gaunt structure of the Upper Shoots beacon, on the approach to the Severn Suspension Bridge. This beacon marks the west side of the English Stones reef and should be left a good cable to starboard going up-channel.

Severn suspension bridge. Now the stream will be more or less behind you. At this point, yachts with VHF should establish contact with Sharpness Radio.

Chapel Rock lighthouse, on an islet just beyond the entrance to the River Wye, should be left between $\frac{1}{4}$ and $\frac{1}{2}$ mile to port so that you are positioned well in mid-stream. Once abreast Chapel Rock make for the quick flashing blue light under the centre span of the bridge. The current is often turbulent around the bridge as it surges through the narrows over an uneven bottom: plenty of power and some attentive steering are usually needed. Once under the bridge come round steadily to port to leave Lyde Rock beacon about 100m to the SW, heading NW then N so as to tuck close under Beachley Point into Slime Road.

Follow round past the prominent red cliffs at Sedbury keeping $1\frac{1}{2}$–2 cables off the bank. Slime Road white daymarks and fixed blue leading lights will now be close astern. Off Inward Rocks Point, $2\frac{1}{2}$ miles above the bridge, alter to the ENE so as to leave Counts N-cardinal light-float a cable to starboard, making towards a conspicuous white house on the E shore.

Soon after passing the Counts you will leave two beacon structures about 2 cables to starboard: the northernmost of these stands on the N wall of the tidal reservoir that helps cool Oldbury nuclear power station. This large walled lake is submerged above half-tide and should always be given a good berth. The two beacon structures form the next leading line to the NE; follow their transit (back bearing 233°Mag.) as far as Hills Flats light-float, which should be left $1\frac{1}{2}$ cables to starboard.

After passing Hills Flats, make good about 065°Mag. for a mile and then turn to make good 085°Mag., leaving Hayward Rock light float close to starboard and picking up the fixed blue Conigre leading lights. When about $\frac{1}{4}$ mile from the E bank, come back to the NE so as to leave Berkeley Power Station baffle wall and its three beacon structures a good cable to starboard, keeping Fishing House fixed white leading lights in line astern. The baffle wall is about 400m long and covers near HW.

Just beyond the N end of the baffle wall is Bull Rock and its beacon, best left about 20m to starboard. Note that coasters sometimes pass to the E of Bull Rock when bound down-river against the last of the flood. Keep about 300m off the bank as you pass the narrow entrance to Berkeley Pill and the shallow inlet of Panthurst Pill. You'll see Sharpness pierheads jutting out from the E shore, about a mile upstream from Berkeley Pill.

On the bank just beyond Panthurst Pill is a fixed blue light, known locally as the 'swinging light'. At this point it is usually a good plan to round up into the tide and then drop astern towards the pierheads, keeping control by running slow ahead. Ships may be locking out as you arrive so call Sharpness Radio for instructions. If you don't have VHF, edge towards the entrance and watch for the docking signals: 2 black balls or 2 red lights mean that the dock is closed; 1 black ball or 1 red light means that the entrance is not clear; a green flag over a black ball, or a green light over a red, means that you may enter, with small craft docking before larger vessels. If no signals are showing and all seems clear, go into the outer basin, secure alongside and await directions.

Sharpness locks are worked for about $1\frac{1}{2}$ hr before local HW, and after HW only as commercial traffic dictates. Having locked in yachts should pass through the docks, negotiate the two swing bridges and then turn hard-a-port into a cut where Sharpness Marine have their pleasant bankside berths. This quiet backwater was the original lock basin between the Severn and the

Charston Rock lighthouse, which lies at the north end of The Shoots channel and is left $1\frac{1}{2}$ cables to port on the passage upstream towards the Severn Suspension Bridge.

The approach to the Severn Suspension Bridge, showing the west support tower and chapel rock with its beacon. Chapel Rock is left between $\frac{1}{4}$ and $\frac{1}{2}$ mile to port on the way upstream.

Chapel Rock and its beacon, which lie on the north side of the Severn Estuary just below the suspension bridge. The beacon is shown closer here than you should approach it in practice.

Gloucester-Sharpness Canal, before the docks were built in the 1870s. The canal still carries commercial shipping and increasing numbers of pleasure craft. Beyond Gloucester even quite deep-draft yachts can rejoin the Severn just below Ashleworth. The canalised river can take you up to Tewkesbury, Upton-upon-Severn and the attractive old city of Worcester.

Yachts outward bound from Sharpness should aim to lock out about $\frac{1}{2}$ hr before HW there, taking some foul tide on the downward passage to start with. Follow the up-river directions in reverse, but remember that at HW Sharpness the tide will have been ebbing in The Shoots for nearly $\frac{3}{4}$ hr: by the time you get down below the Severn Bridge the ebb will be running strongly. Once you have passed Charston lighthouse take care to stay in the deep-water channel, and beware being set westwards towards Lady Bench and Gruggy shoals.

Sharpness

Summary Sharpness lies on the E bank of the Severn, about 9 miles above the Severn Bridge. Sharpness Docks are still active and are situated at the seaward end of the Gloucester & Berkeley Canal, which bypasses the shallow, higher reaches of the tidal Severn. Sharpness is an interesting haven in its own right, but is also the gateway to the SW Midlands inland waterways; from here, quite deep-draft yachts can penetrate inland as far as Worcester. Entry to Sharpness is via a tidal lock accessible for about $1\frac{1}{2}$ hr before HW. Once inside pass through the docks, negotiate two swing bridges and turn to port into the cut where Sharpness Marine have their attractive visitors' berths.

Tides HW Sharpness is at HW Avonmouth +00hr 40min, or HW Dover −03hr 35min. Heights above chart datum: 9.3m MHWS, 0.5m MLWS, 5.8m MHWN, 0.2m MLWN.

Port Control Gloucester Harbour Trustees. Contact Sharpness Radio (VHF Ch 16, working Ch 14) as you leave Avonmouth and again near the Severn Bridge.

Tidal streams and currents

The river ebb starts running soon after local HW and the flood soon after local LW. Streams are strong, up to 5 knots at springs. Beware the cross-set when entering between Sharpness pierheads.

Description

Sharpness is an old established port whose importance grew steadily after the completion of the Gloucester & Berkeley ship canal in 1827. This waterway was built to bypass the tortuous higher stretches of the tidal Severn above Sharpness Point, enabling large ocean-going ships to make the inland passage up to Gloucester. The original entrance locks led into the now tranquil backwater where Sharpness Marine have their moorings.

Sharpness 'New Dock' was opened in 1874, together with a new and larger canal entrance $\frac{1}{2}$ mile further downstream. The port has since seen ebbs and flows in its fortunes, but it is still active and remains the headquarters for the

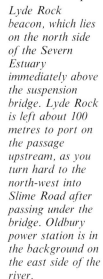

Lyde Rock beacon, which lies on the north side of the Severn Estuary immediately above the suspension bridge. Lyde Rock is left about 100 metres to port on the passage upstream, as you turn hard to the north-west into Slime Road after passing under the bridge. Oldbury power station is in the background on the east side of the river.

The Severn Estuary above the suspension bridge near low water, looking north west towards Slime Road.

Berkeley power station is conspicuous on the east side of the Severn about 1½ miles below Sharpness pierheads. You leave it close to starboard on the way upstream.

Severn Pilots. Pleasure boat traffic on the canal now increases steadily each year and the trip inland to Gloucester and beyond is most picturesque. Deep-draft yachts can penetrate as far as Worcester where there is a sheltered and attractive basin suitable for laying-up.

The passage up the Severn from Avonmouth to Sharpness is tricky, and needs to be timed carefully for the last part of the flood. Sharpness locks will admit yachts for about $1\frac{1}{2}$ hr before HW and Sharpness Radio controls traffic approaching the port. The lock foreman, Mervin Nash, is very helpful to yachtsmen. Inside the harbour, beyond the docks, the visitors' berths at Sharpness Marine are quiet and sheltered, a pleasant spot for a couple of days' stay. The town of Sharpness is a short walk from the docks area and offers reasonable shopping.

Outer approaches and entry

Follow the directions for the Upper Severn from Avonmouth to Sharpness (see pages 74ff). It is possible to reach Sharpness at night, since all the leading lines in this stretch of the river are lit, but night navigation is not recommended to anyone without either local knowledge or a pilot.

Berths and anchorages

Sharpness Marine These peaceful canalside berths are situated in what was once the original lock basin between the Severn and the Gloucester & Berkeley Canal. This stretch of deep water, now a cul-de-sac, is entered by passing from the present tidal lock through Sharpness Docks, negotiating two swing bridges, and then turning hard to port. Sharpness Marine have good facilities and you can obtain diesel, Calor gas, chandlery, fresh water and electricity. You can contact the proprietor, John Hobson, in advance on Dursley (0453) 811476. Boats can safely be left here unattended.

Sharpness Docks Boats can be moored in the Docks by arrangement with the lock master, but the berthing is less congenial than at Sharpness Marine.

Anchorages There are no safe anchorages in the River Severn near Sharpness.

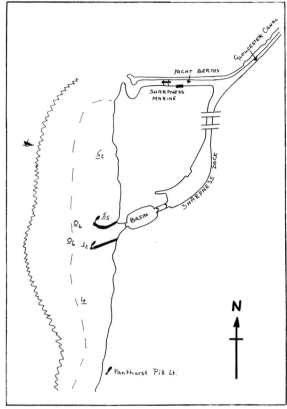

Sharpness

Oldbury Pill

A narrow inlet on the E side of the River Severn, $2\frac{1}{2}$ miles above the Severn Bridge and nearly a mile downstream from Oldbury Power Station. Thornbury Sailing Club is at the mouth of the pill, where there is also a fixed jetty. Further in, you will find a floating jetty, a slip and some local moorings. The pill is accessible for $2\frac{1}{2}$ hr either side of local HW, which is about 20 min after HW Avonmouth.

Coming up-Channel, pass under the centre of the Severn Bridge and make good 075°Mag. towards a red-brick chimney behind Littleton Pill. When about 2 cables off the shore stay parallel with it to avoid various salmon weirs. Oldbury Pill lies a mile upstream from the chimney, and the sailing club and jetty are conspicuous on its N side. When the pill is open, turn into the entrance leaving a small buoy and the jetty close to port. Continue up the N side of the pill, leaving to starboard the moorings off the S side. Fetch up just before a floating jetty attached to the N bank; at LW keelboats can sit upright here in soft mud. Do not venture beyond this jetty, where there are many dinghy moorings.

Coming down-Channel, leave Sharpness an hour before HW there and follow the Upper Severn directions as far as the Counts light-float. Provided you reach this mark by 1 hr after HW Oldbury, turn **to steer** about 145°Mag.

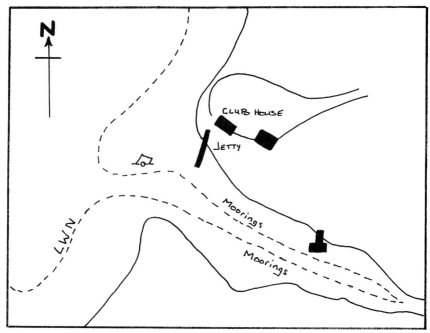

Oldbury Pill

The alongside berths run by Sharpness Marine are perfectly sheltered and you can obtain Calor gas, chandlery, fresh water and electricity.

towards a prominent tree plantation just S of Oldbury Power Station: the ebb will keep you clear of the cooling reservoir and carry you down towards the pill.

The River Avon and Bristol

Summary The mouth of Bristol's River Avon lies close S of Avonmouth south pierhead and ½ mile NE of the entrance to Royal Portbury Dock. Avonmouth and Royal Portbury are commercial docks which are normally prohibited to yachts: keep clear of shipping in their approaches. The Avon practically dries at LW to thick mud, but is navigable above half-tide for the 6 miles to Bristol. Visitors to Bristol lock into the City Docks where there is a marina. There are drying berths at Pill Creek 2 miles up the Avon. Yachts waiting for sufficient rise of tide to enter the river can anchor in Portishead Pool 1½ miles WSW of the entrance.

Tides HW Avonmouth is at HW Dover −4hr 15min. Heights above chart datum: 13.2m MHWS, 0.9m MLWS, 10.0m MHWN, 3.5m MLWN. HW at Bristol is 10min after HW Avonmouth.

Port Control Port of Bristol Authority. Call Avonmouth Radio as you approach the Avon, and City Docks Radio once you are well up-river just before Avon Gorge. Call on VHF Ch 16, working low power Ch 12 and 14.

Tidal streams and currents

Streams are strong in the approaches to Avonmouth, in excess of 5 knots on a spring flood. The tide is also strong in the Avon itself, so it is best not to enter until 2 hr before HW Bristol.

Description

The dockland complexes of Avonmouth and Royal Portbury are conspicuous from the Severn estuary, and somewhere among them is the relatively narrow entrance to the River Avon. The Avon dries out at LWS, but is navigable on the tide for the 6 miles to the city of Bristol. The upper part of this passage leads through the dramatic Avon Gorge and under the elegant Clifton Suspension Bridge. Take care not to obstruct any shipping using the fairway.

The two pierhead lighthouses at the entrance to Avonmouth Docks. The mouth of the River Avon lies close south of the south pier, on the far right of the picture.

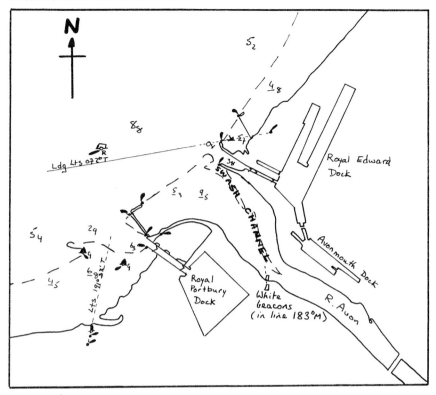

Avonmouth

Pill Creek, a sheltered drying inlet off the S side of the River Avon, about ½ mile above the M5 flyover. Enter within 1½ hr of local HW, leaving the moored boats in the centre of the Pill to starboard.

Visitors to Bristol must lock into the City Docks, whose entrance is on the N side of the river about $\frac{1}{4}$ mile above the suspension bridge. Bristol Marina lies on the S side of what is known as the Floating Harbour, the docks' main inner basin, but you have to pass through Cumberland Basin first. About $\frac{1}{2}$ mile into the Floating Harbour you will see the pontoon berths to starboard, just before the drydock containing *SS Great Britain*. The marina has all the usual facilities, with a boatyard, chandlery and marine engineers on site.

Pill Creek, which dries completely to soft mud, lies on the S side of the Avon, 2 miles up from Avonmouth and $\frac{1}{2}$ mile above the M5 flyover. This tranquil backwater provides a retreat from the fast-flowing river and offers perfect shelter in any weather. At the head of the inlet is a small common with shops nearby. Members of Portishead Cruising Club have their moorings here, and the clubhouse and slip is on the W bank of the entrance. There is an iron jetty and a drying grid in the SE corner of the pill.

Outer approaches

Approaching the mouth of the Avon involves negotiating some of the fastest flowing stretches of the Severn estuary and avoiding various extensive areas of drying sand and mud. The tide is a critical factor, whether you are coming upstream or downstream. The good news is that the approaches to the Avon are well marked, because of the considerable volume of commerical traffic using these waters, but keep well clear of any shipping manoeuvring in the vicinity of Avonmouth. Admiralty chart 1859 is highly recommended.

Coming upstream from seaward, Bristol Deep is the buoyed fairway which follows the S shore of the Severn and leads broadly ENE from the English and Welsh Grounds light-float (LFl, 10s, red hull with white lettering). The float is moored between these two shoal areas at a natural 'crossroads' in the estuary, 5 miles S by W from the mouth of the River Usk and 6 miles NE of Flat Holm.

If you are bound straight up the Avon for Bristol it is usually best to arrive off the English and Welsh Grounds about 3 hr before HW Avonmouth. This gives you, say, just over an hour to cover the 11 miles to Avonmouth (normally plenty of time with the powerful flood tide under you), and a similar period to make the passage up the Avon to the docks entrance, arriving at least $\frac{1}{2}$ hr before HW so as to catch the last inward lock opening.

From the light-float, make good just N of E for 2 miles to the North Elbow green conical bell buoy (QG), leaving it to starboard. On this leg the tide will be coming from over your starboard quarter. Continue E by N for nearly 2 miles to Clevedon N-cardinal buoy (VQ), and for a further $1\frac{1}{2}$ miles to Avon green conical (FlG, 2.5s). The stream will now be right behind you, following the line of the river. Now start to close the S shore slightly, heading for a position $\frac{1}{4}$ mile off Black Nore Point.

From Black Nore, aim to pass about a cable off Portishead Point, with its two conspicuous power station chimneys. Then make for the Firefly green conical bell buoy, $\frac{3}{4}$ mile ENE of Portishead Point, leaving it close to starboard. The entrance to the Avon lies not quite $1\frac{1}{2}$ miles 080° Mag. from the Firefly buoy, leaving Cockburn Shoal red can buoy (FlR) about 2 cables to port.

Coming down the Severn via The Shoots, say from Sharpness or St Pierre Pill, follow the Avonmouth-Sharpness directions in reverse (see pages 74ff). The trouble with this passage is that you will have used up 2–3 hr of ebb by the time you arrive off Avonmouth, so the stream will be foul in the Avon with the river level falling quickly. The best plan is to continue $1\frac{1}{2}$ miles downstream to Portishead, leaving Cockburn red can buoy to starboard and making for the two conspicuous chimneys. Anchor at Portishead Pool until about 2 hr before the next HW (see page 89), when the Avon may be entered safely.

Entry

It is important to allow for cross-tide on the final approach. If you have VHF call Avonmouth Radio on Ch 16 (working low power Ch 12 or 14) to advise them of your destination. The mouth of the Avon is effectively 4 cables wide between Avonmouth south pierhead (OcRG) with its prominent signal station and the Royal Portbury Docks pier end (LFlG, 15s). There is a shoal area in the entrance; the deepest water lies in the Swash Channel over on the N side for the first $\frac{1}{4}$ mile, close to Avonmouth south pier.

When St George's leading marks come into line—two white columns on the S side of the river bearing 183°Mag. (both Oc, 5s)— follow their transit until you are close to the bank. The channel then curves back across to the N side of the river before generally following the middle, but tending towards the outside of bends. There are several other pairs of white column leading marks on the way up to Bristol, all of them lit. Pill Creek lies on the S side of the river $\frac{1}{2}$ mile above the M5 flyover. Enter within $1\frac{1}{2}$ hr of HW, leaving the moored boats in the centre of the pill to starboard.

If bound for Bristol, call City Docks Radio on Ch 16 (working Ch 12 or 14) before you reach the Avon Gorge. The entrance lock is not far beyond the suspension bridge to port. A watch is kept from 3 hr before to 1 hr after local

Bristol marina is situated on the S side of the 'Floating Harbour', between the Baltic Wharf development and SS Great Britain. There is complete shelter here, with ready access to boatyard facilities, engineers and chandlery.

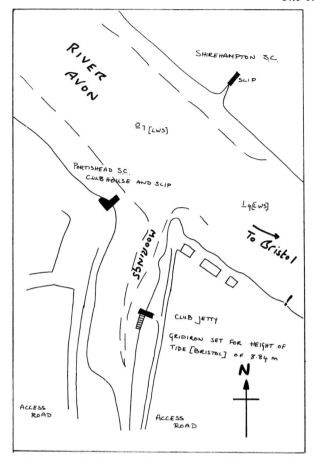

RIVER AVON

SHIREHAMPTON S.C.

SLIP

○7 [LWS]

PORTISHEAD S.C.
CLUB HOUSE AND SLIP

⊥9[EWS]

To Bristol

MOORINGS

CLUB JETTY

GRIDIRON SET FOR HEIGHT OF
TIDE [BRISTOL] OF 8.84 m

N

ACCESS
ROAD

ACCESS
ROAD

Avon Pill

HW, although lockings do not normally occur after HW. Inward locking times are currently 2hr 35min, 1hr 25min and 15min before HW. The lock stays open for $\frac{1}{2}$ hr after these times if other craft are expected.

If you arrive early for locking-in, go alongside Hotwells Pontoon a little way below the lock entrance. Contact the Dock Master on VHF Ch 16 (low power) and/or wait until you get a green light on the pontoon signal mast. When in the lock keep to the outer end, away from the worst of the sluice turbulence. If you arrive too late for the lock, you can either: go back down the river to Pill; dry out on a gridiron a little way upsteam from the lock entrance, flanked by four wooden dolphins; take the mud alongside the N wall, just downstream from the lock and *no closer* to it than 'No. 4' survey mark; or stay alongside the pontoon and go aground in the soft mud.

Having locked into Cumberland Basin and passed through the entrance lock swing bridge, you then have to negotiate a second swing bridge at the 'Junction Lock' between the basin and the Floating Harbour. Sound Morse code A for the bridge to be opened. Bristol Marina lies about $\frac{1}{2}$ mile into the Floating Harbour on the starboard hand.

Anyone intending to visit Bristol is advised to obtain the useful booklet compiled by the port authority called *Information for Owners of Pleasure Craft*, which contains locking times and all other necessary information about the docks. It is available by post from: Harbour Master's Office, Underfall Yard, Cumberland Rd, Bristol BS1 6XG—tel (0272) 24797 or 25381.

Entry at night

This is not recommended for strangers, but is quite feasible using Admiralty chart 1859. The leading marks in the River Avon are all lit, and there are also numerous single lights on either bank—green lights to starboard and orange lights to port.

Berths and anchorages

Bristol Marina Situated on the S side of the Floating Harbour, between the Baltic Wharf development and *SS Great Britain*, the marina's pontoon berths offer complete shelter with ready access to boatyard facilities, engineers and chandlery. Diesel and water are available alongside. The marina is about a mile from the city centre but there are shops within a short walking distance.

Pill Creek This attractive drying inlet off the S side of the Avon is the headquarters of Portishead Cruising Club, who welcome visitors. It is a good idea to contact the secretary in advance at: The Clubhouse, Pump Square, Pill, Bristol BS20 0BG. Enter near HW if possible, or at least within $1\frac{1}{2}$ hr of HW. You take the ground in soft mud, whether you use a vacant mooring or go alongside the iron jetty in the SE corner of the pill. There is a water tap close to the jetty and local shops nearby.

The River Avon It is possible to anchor in the lower reaches in case of an emergency, but this is discouraged because of shipping using the fairway. Good ground tackle is required because the stream in the Avon is strong, up to 5 knots at springs.

The upper Avon to Clifton Suspension Bridge

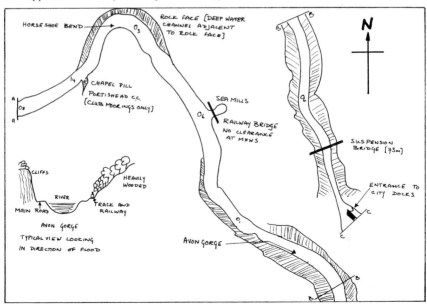

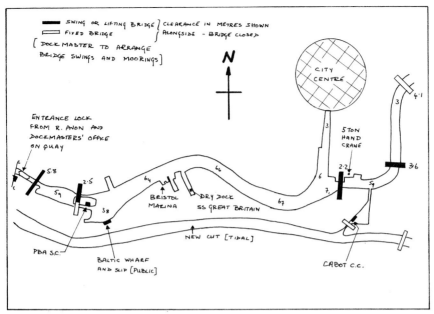

Bristol Docks (courtesy of Bristol Channel Yachting Conference)

Portishead

Summary Portishead Dock, whose entrance lies $1\frac{1}{2}$ miles WSW of the mouth of the Avon, is practically derelict and is closed to yachts except in an emergency. But Portishead Pool, partially protected by a pier just outside the dock, offers an anchorage sheltered from W through S to SE. At springs most of the pool dries to soft mud into which keelboats can settle. Yachts should neither moor alongside nor anchor too close to the pier, where the bottom is uneven with stones. The pool is a handy staging post for yachts waiting to proceed further up the Severn, or up the Avon to Bristol or Pill.

Tides HW Portishead is at HW Dover -4hr 15min, i.e. at the same time as HW Avonmouth. Heights above chart datum in Portishead Pool: 13.1m MHWS and 9.9m MHWN.

Port Control Port of Bristol Authority. In an emergency call Portishead Dock Radio on VHF Ch 16 (working 12 or 14) from $2\frac{1}{2}$ hr before to $1\frac{1}{2}$ hr after HW.

Tidal streams and currents

Streams are moderate in the bay between Portishead pier and Royal Portbury Dock, but strong further out in King Road. A local eddy sets W towards the pierhead for most of the flood. Close inshore off Portishead Point, the stream turns W-going 2 hr before HW.

Description

Once an active trading port, Portishead has been steadily eclipsed by Avonmouth and Royal Portbury. Portishead dock is now very run down, being used only occasionally by bauxite ships importing ore to a local smelter. A handful of local yachts lay-up there during the winter. Other yachts *can* enter the dock near HW, in an emergency only and with some advance warning.

Portishead is easily identified from the Severn estuary by two tall chimneys above the power station situated on the W side of the dock entrance lock. The entrance faces NE but is sheltered from the N and W by a quay and then a pier. The area immediately outside the lock gates is known as Portishead Pool. It was once a pool proper, scoured by a drainage sluice serving the low-lying land to the S, but it now dries for about 2 hr either side of LW. However, the soft mud is quite safe for a keelboat to sink into, and the 'pool' makes a useful passage anchorage for those waiting for sufficient rise of tide to proceed further up the Severn or enter the Avon.

There are a few local moorings in 'the Hole' on the S side of the pool, although there are no facilities nearby. You may land at the pier when the tide serves. A footpath leads in behind the power station to Portishead, but the shops are some distance away. There is a water tap near the lock keeper's office.

Portishead Pool

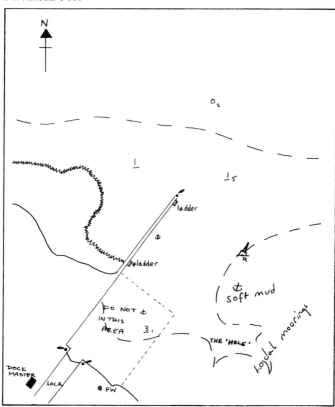

Approach and entry

Coming up the estuary, follow the directions for Avonmouth, but come onto about due S Mag. after rounding Firefly green conical bell buoy (Fl2G). Firefly rocks (0.9m) lie about ½ cable S by W of the buoy, so make for a position a good cable E of Portishead pierhead (IsoG, 2s). Watch for the W-going eddy setting towards the pier. Head SW into the pool when the dock entrance opens up, leaving the pier to starboard and Portishead red can buoy (FlR, 5s) to port; the buoy marks the edge of a shallow bank.

Coming down the estuary, stay out in the main channel as far as Royal Portbury Outer green conical buoy (IQG, 12s). Thence turn SW between Portishead pierhead and the red can buoy as before.

Entry at night

Portishead can be approached at night near HW, so long as you take care to counteract first the main tidal stream and then the eddy. In addition to the lit marks detailed above, there are also lights either side of the lock entrance: 2FR(vert) on the E wall and 2FG(vert) on the W. Signal lights may be shown by day or night when a ship is due to enter the dock. Banks of red and green horizontal fluorescent tubes at the root of Portishead pier are lit as follows: red lights—not clear to enter, vessels must remain in King Road; green lights—vessels may approach the entrance lock.

Berths and anchorages

Portishead Pool Anchor in line with the lock entrance, abreast the *timber* section of the pier immediately opposite the steps. You will sit in soft mud for about 2 hr either side of LW, but before drying out check with the lock keeper

Local moorings at Portishead Pool in the shadow of the power station.

that no ships are expected. This anchorage is sheltered from W through S to SE, but is very choppy in fresh winds from between N and NE.

In quiet weather, and preferably at neaps, you can stay afloat by anchoring in 3–7m between Firefly and Flatness Rocks, i.e. about 2 cables NE of the pierhead. This position is reasonably sheltered from SW through S to SE.

Portishead Dock Can be entered in an emergency, but a certain amount of notice is required. Contact the lock keeper in person, having anchored in the pool, or call Portishead Dock Radio or Avonmouth Radio on Ch 16 (working 12 or 14).

Redcliff and Walton Bays

Between Black Nore Point and Ladye Point, a distance of not quite 3 miles, there are one or two useful passage anchorages sheltered from the E and S. Depths are moderate, but you need to tuck in as close as possible to avoid the worst of the tide. The coastline of low cliffs is straight and uncomplicated.

Redcliff Bay Only ½ mile SW from Black Nore Point. When edging close in be sure to avoid the various rocky ledges that fringe the foreshore, especially those just to the NE.

Walton (and Charlcombe) Bay A better anchorage is at Walton Bay, midway

Redcliff, Walton and Charlcombe Bays

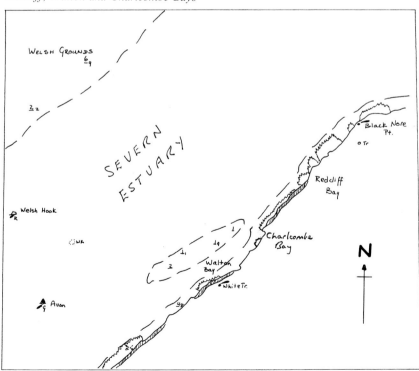

The approach to Clevedon Pill is rather tortuous, but the marshes provide surprisingly good protection once you are safely tucked inside.

between Black Nore Point and Ladye Point and **inside** Walton Sand (dries 2.5m). Walton Bay can easily be located close NE of Walton old signal station, a conspicuous white tower on the cliffs. The tower still exhibits a light (Fl2, 2.5s). Charlcombe Bay lies only ¼ mile NE of Walton Bay and there is a small rocky ledge between them.

Clevedon Pill

Summary This fascinating drying creek about 6 miles SW down the Severn estuary from Portishead provides a base for Clevedon SC. The entrance lies just downstream from Clevedon itself, between prominent Wain's Hill and Spear Rocks to the E and Blackstone Rocks to the W. Strangers should approach within 2 hr of HW, and only then if having no more than 1m draft. The tortuous channel is marked, rather enigmatically, by perches. Near the head of the creek you can find good shelter by taking the ground in the narrow fairway between the salt marshes. Lie either to fore-and-aft anchors or use a vacant local mooring with permission from the club.

Tides HW Clevedon is at HW Dover −4hr 25min, or at HW Avonmouth −00hr 10min. Heights above chart datum: 12.8m MHWS, 0.9m MLWS, 9.8m MHWN, 3.7m MLWN.

Port Control None as such. The moorings in Clevedon Pill are administered by Clevedon Sailing Club.

Tidal streams and currents

Off the entrance, the tide turns 20 min before slack water out in the estuary.

The streams run NE-SW and reach $3\frac{1}{2}$ knots at springs. The last of the flood sets offshore near Blackstone Rocks. The ebb coming down from Walton Bay also tends to set offshore.

Description

Clevedon Pill is a short drying inlet on the S shore of the Severn estuary, roughly midway between Weston-super-Mare and Portishead. Apart from Wain's Hill the coastline here is rather low-lying, close as it is to the Somerset Levels. At the head of Clevedon Pill is a Flemish-looking dyke with a drainage

Clevedon Pill

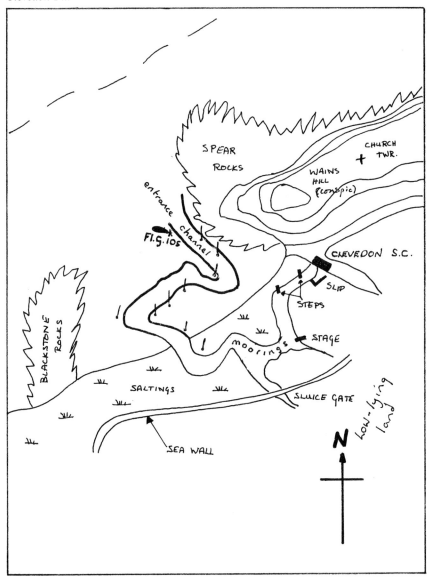

sluice, and the inlet itself is fringed with salt marshes.

The pill is occupied by a good many local boats of mostly shoal draft, and its upper part offers good shelter in almost all conditions. The inlet is only vulnerable at HW springs in a fresh northwesterly; the marshes are then covered and the protection they give to the narrow winding channel is temporarily removed. Clevedon SC at the head of the pill welcomes visitors. There are shops and a garage within ½ mile.

Approach and entry

Coming up the estuary: in quiet weather only, strangers should pass about ¼ mile off Sand Point no earlier than 1½ hr before HW. Then make good 060°Mag., which in practice means heading for the coastline receding beyond Clevedon. This course takes you over Langford Grounds, well covered at this state of tide. Four miles on from Sand Point you'll see Wain's Hill coming up on the starboard bow, but be sure to stay outside Blackstone Rocks by keeping Ladye Point well open of the end of ruined Clevedon Pier.

When Wain's Hill bears 100°Mag. turn straight towards it, but keep clear of Spear Rocks close NW of Wain's Hill, and Blackstone Rocks off the W side of the pill. As you draw inshore you should be able to see the outer post with two smaller perches beyond it. These marks lie close to the W of Wain's Hill. The post, which is lit (FlG, 10s), should be left close to starboard. The two perches are left to port, but the next perch is left to starboard as the channel turns W and then SW, leaving three more perches to port. Opposite the last of these three is another perch on the W side of the channel, marking the point at which the deep water makes a right-angle turn to the SE. Thereafter leave the perches to port and follow up between the salt marshes.

Coming down the estuary: between Portishead and Clevedon the coast is reasonably clear of dangers save for the long sandbank (dries 3m) off Walton Bay. A useful mark is the Avon green conical buoy (FlG, 2.5s) which lies just over a mile N by E from the end of Clevedon Pier. From the Avon buoy make good about 210°Mag. for 2 miles, passing the pier at least 3 cables off. This

There is good shelter for shoal draft boats near the head of Clevedon Pill. Lie to fore-and-aft anchors or use a vacant local mooring with permission from Clevedon Sailing Club.

course takes you to a position close WNW of Wain's Hill, whence you should proceed as above.

Entry at night

Not recommended for strangers. Note that the Clevedon Pill outer post has the same characteristics as Clevedon pierhead (FlG, 10s).

Berths and anchorages

In the Pill Work into the Pill between the salt marshes and look for a clear spot where you can lie in the channel with fore-and-aft anchors which should be buoyed. You should ask at the clubhouse before taking the ground: it is important not to obstruct the fairway, and in any case it may be possible to use a vacant mooring. Wherever you come to rest, be sure to stay well away from the banks: they are steep and you will dry out at an uncomfortable angle if you tuck in too close. There are various small wooden landing stages in the upper part of the pill, and a concrete slip near the clubhouse.

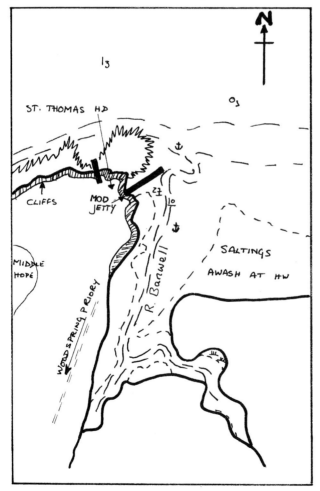

Woodspring Bay

Langford Swatch

In quiet weather Langford Swatch makes an interesting shortcut between
Clevedon and Sand Point, *inside* Langford Grounds. It also provides access to
anchorages in Woodspring Bay. This passage only dries about 5ft at MLWS
and is available for most of the tide at neaps. The streams follow the line of the
Swatch and can reach 3 knots, especially when Langford Grounds are
uncovered.

Coming down-Channel, say from Clevedon Pill, steer SSW from a position
a cable or so off Blackstone Rocks. This course leads between the hard, gently
shoaling sand of Langford Grounds and the steeper mudbank fringing the
coast. Keep towards the mud rather than the sand. About $1\frac{1}{2}$ miles
downstream from Blackstone you will see two above-water wrecks $\frac{1}{4}$ mile off
the beach. Pass close outside these wrecks and follow the trend of the shore.
Off the mouth of the Yeo, steer towards St Thomas's Head when it bears due
W. Clear St Thomas's by 2 cables and then hug Middle Hope along to Sand
Point, continuing no more than 2 cables off.

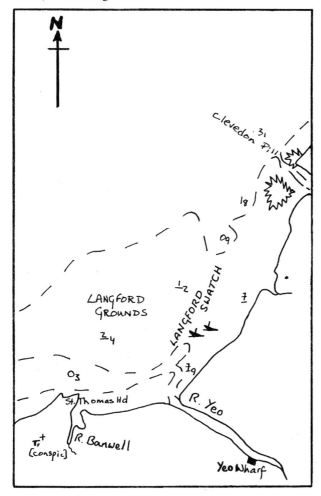

Langford Swatch

Woodspring Bay

In offshore winds there is a passage anchorage off the mouth of the Yeo. Except at low springs you can stay afloat in the Swatch itself, or you can tuck further in out of the tide and sit in the mud. The same applies to the mouth of the Banwell, just SE of St Thomas's Head off the MOD jetty. These are both very peaceful get-away-from-it-all spots, and there are no facilities ashore.

Weston-super-Mare

Summary A busy seaside resort at the N end of Weston Bay. Knightstone harbour lies close SE of Anchor Head which, together with Birnbeck Island, forms the N extremity of the bay. The harbour is rather exposed to the S, partly protected from the SW by its sea wall, and sheltered from other directions by the land. The firm sandy bottom allows keelboats to dry out on legs or against two wooden piles at the quay. Knightstone is accessible for about 2 hr either side of HW, but neaps restrict movements to shoal-draft boats.

Tides HW Weston-super-Mare is at HW Dover −4hr 35min, or HW Avonmouth −00hr 20min. Heights above chart datum: 12.0m MHWS, 0.7m MLWS, 9.0m MHWN, 2.7m MLWN.

Port Control Contact Weston Bay YC, on the seaward side of Knightstone Causeway. They listen on VHF Ch 37(M) at peak periods during the summer.

Tidal streams and currents

There is always a S-going stream in Weston Bay, strongest at half ebb and flood. At the S end of the bay the tide sets W along Brean Down, causing

Knightstone Harbour, Weston-super-Mare, facing WSW. Yachts can dry out on firm ground to the E of the harbour wall. There are numerous mooring chains on the bottom, so anchors should be buoyed. In the centre background you can see the post beacon which marks the end of a short causeway extending from the pierhead.

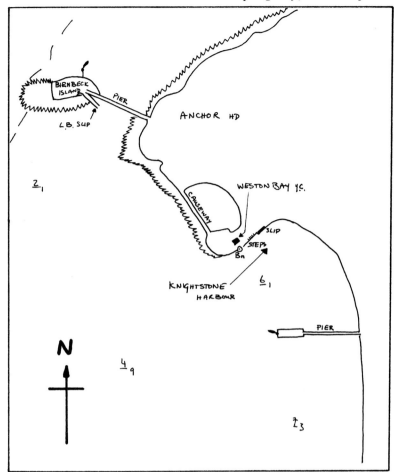

Weston-super-Mare

overfalls off Howe Rock in fresh westerlies. The strong streams off Birnbeck Island can also cause overfalls.

Description

The broad expanse of Weston Bay faces due W and is bounded on the N by Anchor Head and Birnbeck Island, and on the S by the distinctive promontory of Brean Down. The bay dries completely, to sand close in and mud further out. It is fringed by Weston-super-Mare's popular beaches. Tucked into the NE corner of the bay, close to the town centre, Knightstone harbour is partly protected from the SW by the curve of the sea wall, the SW end of which is referred to below as Knightstone Pier. The harbour has a firm bottom, is reasonably sheltered except between S and SW, and can generally be entered 2 hr either side of HW.

Two cables S of the harbour is Weston Grand Pier, a prominent mark from offshore and left well to starboard on the way in. The pier acts as a partial breakwater from the S and should not be approached too closely because the tide sets strongly through it. Weston, as it is a bustling seaside resort, is not one of the more tranquil havens of the Bristol Channel. However it does have all the facilities of a large town and its summer holiday atmosphere can be infectious.

Outer approaches

Four miles out in the Bristol Channel, opposite Weston Bay, are the two islands of Flat Holm and Steep Holm. Flat Holm has a lighthouse (Fl3WR, 10s) and several old farm buildings. Steep Holm is maintained as a nature reserve and is unlit. Both are steep-to and can be approached safely provided that due allowance is made for the strong tidal streams out in mid-channel. From Steep Holm, Brean Down bears about 110°Mag. distant $2\frac{3}{4}$ miles, and the entrance to Knightstone Harbour bears nearly due E Mag. distant $4\frac{1}{2}$ miles.

Four miles SW from Steep Holm is the East Culver E-cardinal buoy (Q3, 10s). This marks the E end of the Culver Sand, a narrow shoal more than 3 miles long and drying 4m at its shallowest part. Take care to give this sandbank a good berth when approaching Weston from down-Channel. The West Culver W-cardinal buoy (VQ9, 10s) lies 5 miles WSW from the East Culver buoy.

Approach and entry

Strangers should only approach Weston Bay near HW, preferably on the flood.

From down-Channel, clear Brean Down by at least $\frac{1}{2}$ mile to avoid the overfalls off its W tip. Then head NE for Anchor Head, keeping Birnbeck Island on your port bow and Weston Grand Pier fine to starboard. When entering Weston Bay remember that the stream will begin to set S as you draw inside Birnbeck. The final approach is due E Mag., between Weston Grand Pier to starboard and Knightstone Pier to port. A post beacon marks the end of a short causeway extending from Knightstone pierhead. Round up into the harbour, and either anchor or go alongside the quay.

Coming from up-Channel, give a good berth to Birnbeck Island with its overfalls and strong tidal sets. Then make to the SE to round Anchor Head and Knightstone Pier as above.

Entry at night

Remember that Steep Holm and Brean Down are unlit. The pier on the N side of Birnbeck Island sometimes shows lights (2FG, vert), but don't confuse Birnbeck with Weston Pier (see below). It is important to keep a close watch on your tidal set by taking frequent bearings of lights that you can readily identify, viz: Flat Holm island (Fl3WR, 10s); South Patches isolated danger bell-buoy (Fl2, 5s), which marks a small shoal with 4.3m over it, $1\frac{1}{2}$ miles E by N from Steep Holm; and Weston Grand Pier (2FG, vert).

Berths and anchorages

Knightstone Harbour Yachts can dry out on a firm bottom E of Knightstone pierhead. There are numerous mooring chains in the harbour so anchors should be buoyed. Keelboats may lie alongside the two wooden dolphins at

Local boats dried out in Weston-super-Mare's Knightstone Harbour. Weston Grand Pier is in the background.

the quay, by arrangement with Weston Bay YC. Land at the slip or steps, but take care not to obstruct local boatmen. Shops are nearby and the yacht club has fresh water. It welcomes visitors and has the usual facilities.

The Cut, or 'Sound' Shoal-draft boats can anchor just outside the harbour, S of the old pier near the lifeboat house.

Uphill and the River Axe

Summary The shallow River Axe flows into the SE corner of Weston Bay and in reasonable weather is navigable for about 2 hr either side of HW. Approach from a position 4 cables N of Brean Down and the entrance is marked by post beacons. Uphill, a village on the outskirts of Weston, lies on the E side of the Axe. Several sailing clubs are at Uphill Sands, where there are small boats drawn up on the beach and storage huts for gear. The river contains numerous local moorings, especially in the first $\frac{1}{2}$ mile. There are no visitors' berths as such, but one of the clubs can usually find a vacant mooring for a night or two.

Tides As for Weston, i.e. HW at the river mouth is at HW Dover −4hr 35min, or HW Avonmouth −00hr 20min. Heights above datum: 12.0m MHWS, 0.7m MLWS, 9.0m MHWN, 2.7m MLWN.

Port Control Various local clubs share the organisation of moorings and facilities, viz: Axe SC, Cedar SC, Pegasus SC and Uphill Boat Owners Association.

Tidal streams and currents

The stream is always S-going in Weston Bay, turning W-going along the N shore of Brean Down. There are often overfalls off the W tip of Brean, where this current meets the main Channel tide.

Description

The River Axe is narrow, shallow and muddy, but has a rather wild, salty and attractive atmosphere. It is well packed with boats of all sorts and several sailing clubs are based at Uphill Sands on the E bank. This SE corner of Weston Bay is dominated by Brean Down, a long narrow peninsula with two distinctive 'humps' which forms the S arm of the bay. Brean looks like an island from a distance, since the surrounding land is low-lying.

About ½ mile up the Axe a small tributary known as Uphill Pill joins the main river. The pill winds a short way northwards through the salt-marshes, as far as the Uphill Boat Centre. This busy little yard has a good range of facilities and can handle boats up to 14m l.o.a. and 12 tons dwt; it can be reached near HW. Uphill village, only a short walk from anywhere on the Axe, has several shops and a couple of pubs.

Approach and entry

Coming into Weston Bay first make for the N side of Brean Down, steering for the 'saddle' between its two humps. About 4 cables N of Brean, opposite the saddle, a locally maintained buoy marks the bar of the River Axe. This buoy, called 'Juicy', should be passed close-to. Now identify Black Rock, an above-water rock right in the SE corner of the bay at the mouth of the river.

Bring Black Rock into line with a white mark on Uphill Cliffs. This transit bears about 137°Mag. and should be held as far as the first port-hand mark, a

The River Axe flows into the SE corner of Weston Bay and is navigable for about 2 hr either side of HW in reasonable weather. There are numerous local moorings in the river, especially in the first ½ mile, but they all dry out as shown here.

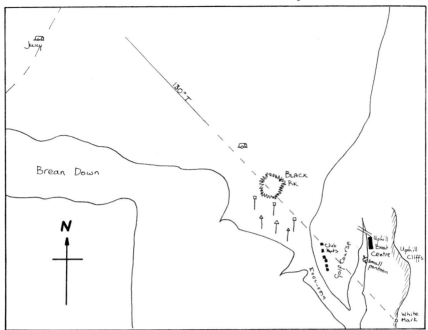

Uphill and the River Axe

barrel with a red top, not quite $\frac{1}{2}$ mile away. If the barrel is not in position approach Black Rock on the transit to within a cable. Enter the river by making a short dog's-leg to the SSE, leaving the rock further to port than Brean Down to starboard. Thereafter follow the line of the port and starboard-hand posts.

Although locals will approach the Axe soon after half-flood, strangers ought to wait until $1\frac{1}{2}$ hr before HW. Entry on the ebb is not advisable; you'll meet a fast current coming out! Fresh winds from between N and NW can kick up a nasty sea on the bar. In strong southerlies, savage down-draughts are often experienced from Brean Down.

Entry at night

Not recommended for strangers.

Berths and anchorages

River Axe Dry out in the soft mud, but don't lie too close to the steep banks. It's best not to anchor, because of the numerous ground chains. Secure to a vacant mooring initially and then ask at one of the clubs. Once safely inside the Axe offers good shelter in all conditions, especially further upstream.

Uphill Pill This narrow creek is used for craft bound to or from Uphill Boat Centre. However, just below the yard there are a few drying pontoon berths to which visitors may sometimes moor.

Close N of Brean Down In moderate winds from between WSW and S there is a reasonable anchorage in a shallow bay on the N side of Brean Down, about 4 cables E of the old fort.

Admiral's Wharf, the new marina complex at Bridgewater. The marina is entered from the River Parrett through a lock to the outer dock then the Bascule Bridge is opened to give access to the marina. The Newtown lock into the Bridgewater–Taunton canal is scheduled to re-open early in 1989.

Uphill Pill is a narrow tributary of the River Axe, used mostly by craft bound to or from Uphill Boat Centre. Just below the boatyard are a few drying pontoon berths, to which visitors may sometimes moor.

Burnham-on-Sea

Summary Situated at the head of Bridgwater Bay, Burnham-on-Sea is approached across a bar nearly 4 miles offshore and thence between the extensive drying banks known as Gore Sand and Stert Flats. The coastline is flat, featureless and rather bleak. A buoyed channel and leading marks are maintained for the coasters that ply up the River Parrett as far as Dunball. Strangers should only approach Burnham in settled offshore weather, but once you are tucked in behind Stert Island a selection of possible berths offers shelter in any conditions.

Tides HW Burnham (or Bridgwater) is at HW Dover -4hr 35min, or HW Avonmouth -00hr 20min. HW Bridgwater Bar is about 10min earlier. Heights above chart datum at Burnham: 10.9m MHWS, $-$**0.2m** MLWS, 8.1m MHWN, 2.1m MLWN.

Port Control Contact Bridgwater Pilots on VHF Ch 16, working Ch 9 or 12.

Tidal streams and currents

The streams flow roughly NE–SW in the offing outside Gore Sand, reaching $3\frac{1}{2}$ knots at springs. Further inshore, towards Burnham, the flows into and out of the River Parrett are more discernible; below half-tide these tend to follow the line of the channel.

Description

Stretching nearly 8 miles SSW from Brean Down are the rather hazardous wastes of Bridgwater Bay, where drying banks of sand and mud reach out for up to 5 miles from a low, featureless shore. The only notable mark inland is Brent Knoll, a conical hill 133m high which is probably more familiar to users of the M5 motorway than to wayward mariners. Conspicuous in the SW corner of the bay is the power station at Hinkley Point. The whole area should be avoided in any fresh W or NW winds, or in poor visibility.

The small seaside town of Burnham-on-Sea is situated at the head of Bridgwater Bay, partly sheltered from the W by a narrow off-lying dune known as Stert Island. There is a drying anchorage between the dune and the shore. The river Parrett joins the sea at Burnham, having wound its way 8 miles down from Bridgwater. There is now an attractive marina at Bridgwater Dock, which makes the rather bleak trip upriver worthwhile. There are various drying anchorages in the Parrett between Burnham and Combwich.

The narrow River Brue joins the sea at Pillsmouth, close S of Burnham. Keelboats can find perfect shelter by drying out in soft mud in the lower reaches of the Brue. Highbridge, about a mile upstream, can be reached near HW. Burnham-on-Sea Yacht Club welcomes visitors to their premises at Pillsmouth, on the N bank.

Outer approaches

In the offing are Steep Holm (unlit) $2\frac{3}{4}$ miles WNW of Brean Down, and Culver Sand (see Weston *outer approaches*). The safest approach to Bridgwater Bay is via the Gore spherical bell-buoy (RWVS, Iso5s), a safe water mark lying $1\frac{3}{4}$ miles NW of Hinkley Point, 4 miles S by E from the East Culver buoy and nearly 7 miles 121°Mag. from the West Culver buoy. Allow for the strong tidal streams when trying to locate the Gore and only proceed eastwards beyond the buoy within 2 hr of HW. A weather-going tide, or any fresh onshore wind, can kick up steep seas in the whole of the bay. Gore Sands are hard and grounding is a serious matter.

If foul weather prevents you from crossing the bar and approaching Burnham, it is usually best to make for Barry, which is accessible in most conditions at any stage of tide.

Approach and entry

From down-Channel or via Gore fairway buoy: From $\frac{1}{4}$ mile S of Gore fairway buoy identify Brent Knoll, a prominent conical hill 2 miles inland from Burnham. Bring the Knoll to bear 085°Mag., its summit just open to the S of a white lighthouse with a red stripe (known as Burnham high light). Approach the shore along this line leaving No 1 green conical buoy (unlit) 2 cables to starboard, No 2 red can (QR) a cable to port and No 3 green conical (unlit) close to starboard. Now bring the SW edge of St Andrew's church tower (behind Burnham seafront) into transit with a white mark on the sea wall bearing 120°Mag. This line leaves No 5 (FIG. 5s) and No 9 (unlit) green conicals to starboard. When about 250m offshore, steer S into the pool between Burnham and Stert Island. You can anchor NNW or SW of the beacon marking the end of Burnham jetty.

From up-Channel: Within 2hrs of HW, in good visibility, you can take the

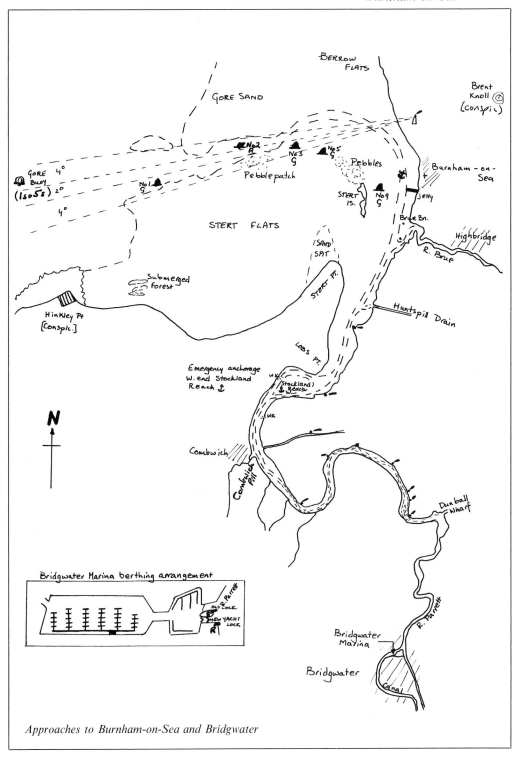

Approaches to Burnham-on-Sea and Bridgwater

107

swatchway through Gore Sand and head straight for No 2 red can buoy from the N. Keep Flatholm lighthouse in line astern with the E end of Steepholm, bearing 172°Mag., and you should pick up No 2 buoy as Brent Knoll begins to bear due E Mag. Leave this buoy about a cable to port, turn towards Brent Knoll and then follow the two leading lines and the buoyed channel as before.

Entry at night

This is not really recommended for strangers although, in fairness, Burnham is one of the better lit approaches along the S shore of the Bristol Channel. The main Burnham-on-Sea entrance lights are shown from a white tower with a red stripe, situated on the foreshore in line with Brent Knoll when bearing due E Mag. The upper light (FlW, 7.5s) is visible between 074° and 164°T. Below this is the directional light (FWRG): its white, safe sector shines over 077°–080°T, with the green sector covering Stert Flats to the S and the red covering Gore Sand to the N.

A pair of inner leading lights (both FR) come into line as you pass No. 5 buoy. This transit bears roughly 102°T, but the front light is moved periodically to meet changes in the channel. Follow these inner leading lights until Huntspill light (FlR, 2s) bears 192°Mag. Head towards Huntspill on this line and anchor E of Stert Island off Burnham seafront.

The River Parrett above Burnham to Bridgwater Marina

Above half-tide the Parrett is navigable for 8 miles as far as Bridgwater, where an attractive marina has been developed in the old dock area at Admirals Wharf. The marina has 175 pontoon berths and visitors are welcome. There is a chandler and engineer on-site, a 30 ton travelift, and a quayside restaurant and pub. Access is by way of a lock, which is not manned unless a vessel is expected—tel Bridgwater (0278) 422222 or try VHF Ch 37(M).

The river flows across the marina lock entrance, making entry difficult except at slack water (which is $\frac{1}{2}$ to 1 hour after HW Bridgwater). Leaving the lock is easier and possible on most tides within 2 hours of HW. During the season there are waiting buoys and a pontoon outside the lock entrance. If you arrive too late to enter the marina, the best berth is in the old ship lock, where keel boats can lie upright in 6ft of silt. The channel to Bridgwater is straightforward—simply keep to the middle, but tend towards the outside of bends. Watch out for coasters leaving or making for the quays at Dunball.

The small village of Combwich lies about halfway up the River Parrett on the W bank. Combwich Cruising Club and Hinkley Point Sailing Club maintain drying moorings in Combwich Pill and can sometimes find a vacant berth for visitors. There are various drying anchorages in the river below Combwich, but tuck well in towards the bank to keep the fairway clear for coasters.

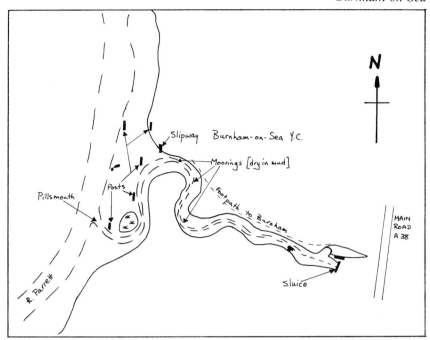

Entrance to River Brue (courtesy of Bristol Channel Yachting Conference)

Berths and anchorages

Off Burnham The area between Burnham seafront and Stert Island doesn't quite dry: two shallow tongues remain, even at MLWS—one off Burnham near the stone jetty and the other further W towards the island. Boats drawing up to 1½m can anchor in either pool and stay afloat around neap tides. Take careful soundings before the tide runs away, though, because the bottom is too soft for using legs but not soft enough for keelboats to settle into. Shoal-draft boats which can take the ground will find good shelter, at springs or neaps, close E of Stert Island and Stert Point. Land at Burnham jetty where the town is close at hand.

River Brue The Brue joins the Parrett at Pillsmouth, ½ mile S by W from Burnham jetty. This narrow river can be entered anytime above half-tide, but the channel is easiest to follow about 2½hr before HW; there is then plenty of depth in the entrance, but the narrow spit extending S by W from near Burnham YC slip will still be visible. To enter the Brue, head S by W from off Burnham jetty, leaving Brue light beacon (QR) close to port. Turn into the river when you come up with a grass-capped islet at the S end of the spit. Leaving the islet and marker posts to port, head back northwards *inside* the spit. Off the YC slip turn E to follow the Brue. Ask at the club for a vacant mooring, or anchor fore-and-aft if you can find room. Buoy your anchors and don't lie too close to the bank. There is shopping at Burnham nearby.

In the River Parrett below Combwich There are various drying anchorages between Stert Point and Combwich. Tuck in close to keep the fairway clear for coasters to or from Dunball.

Combwich Pill Visitors can sometimes use a vacant drying mooring by arrangement with either Combwich CC or Hinkley Point SC. Shops nearby in Combwich village; water and petrol can be obtained from the Harbour Garage at the head of the pill.

Bridgwater Marina The marina offers perfect shelter at peaceful and attractive pontoon berths in the old dock. There is fresh water at the pontoons, with a chandler and marine engineer on site. Bridgwater town centre is close by.

Watchet

Summary A small drying pier harbour situated about 7 miles WSW of Gore fairway buoy and not quite 6 miles ESE of Minehead. It is used by coasters, has a mud bottom and offers good shelter in most weathers. Entry is straightforward within 2 hr of HW and except in fresh onshore winds, but a rocky ledge (dries 3.6m) extends NNW from the W pierhead for almost $\frac{1}{2}$ mile. Visitors should lie alongside the W quay initially and then contact the HM for directions. There is fresh water at the quay, shops are nearby, and the small town is friendly and rather salty.

Tides HW Watchet is at HW Dover -4hr 55min, or HW Avonmouth -00hr 40min. Heights above chart datum: 11.3m MHWS, 1.0m MLWS, 8.5m MHWN, 3.6m MLWN.

Port Control For Watchet harbour call VHF Ch 16 (working 9, 12, or 14) within about 2 hr of HW. You can also telephone in advance on (0984) 31264.

Tidal steams and currents

Off Watchet, the W-going stream begins about $1\frac{1}{4}$ hr after local HW and runs for 5 hr; the E-going stream begins soon after local LW and runs for nearly 7 hr. Rates reach 3 knots at springs and it is important to allow for any cross-tide when entering the harbour.

Description

Watchet is one of the smallest Bristol Channel harbours working commercially and it is fascinating to watch 200ft ships negotiating the narrow entrance, springing through 180° and then fetching up alongside the East Quay. The Channel pilots also use Watchet as the tide serves, so the place often has that busy, rather timeless seafaring atmosphere which attaches to modern ships and high-speed launches as easily as it once did to sailing coasters and pilot cutters.

The twin stone piers overlap to give good shelter in almost all conditions. There are also natural breakwaters provided by the rocky foreshores to the E and W of Watchet, and the drying ledge which extends nearly $\frac{1}{2}$ mile NNW from the W pierhead. The harbour dries to soft mud and a small river feeds into its SW corner, scouring the perimeter with the help of a line of training stakes running parallel with the S wall. The town is nearby and fresh water is available at the quays. The Harbour Master is always very helpful to visiting yachts.

Watchet harbour at low water, looking eastwards towards the commercial quay. You can see the line of training stakes just to the left of the slipway. Coasters still use Watchet regularly, so make sure that the entrance is clear of traffic before coming in or out.

Approach and entry

The outer approaches are straightforward, except that Culver Sand must be avoided when coming across the Bristol Channel from the N and NE, say from Barry or Penarth. The West Culver buoy lies not quite 6 miles due N True from Watchet harbour entrance.

Strangers should only approach Watchet within 2 hr of HW. The lighthouse and flagstaff at the end of the W pier are conspicuous from seaward. Stay at least $\frac{1}{2}$ mile offshore until the pierheads bear about SSW and then head straight for the entrance, allowing for any cross-tide. The ebb stream can be particularly vicious off the W pierhead. Watch out for ships manoeuvring as you come in.

Entry at night

Quite feasible for strangers, provided you are sure of your position in the offing and that you take frequent bearings to assess the tidal set. The W pier lighthouse (FG) has a 9 mile range; the E pierhead light (2FR, vert) has a 3 mile range.

Berths and anchorages

Watchet Harbour Berth alongside the W pier at first and then contact the Harbour Master for directions. Land at either pier, or at the town slipway on the S wall.

Blue Anchor Road This traditional shipping anchorage lies 2–3 miles WNW from Watchet entrance. The broad sweep of Blue Anchor Bay is reasonably sheltered from due W, but open from NW through N to E. Much of it dries at LAT, but edge inshore as far as draft and tide allow. The mud bottom provides good holding.

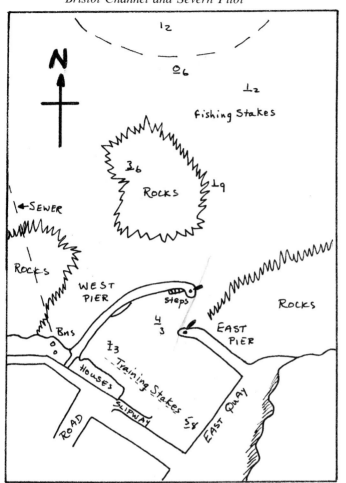

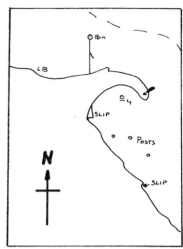

Minehead

Watchet

Blue Anchor Road

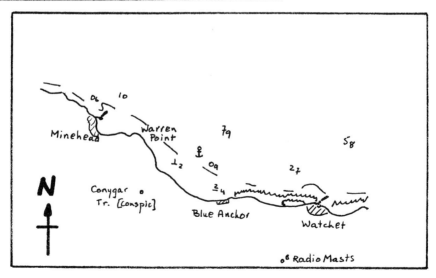

Minehead

Summary Minehead, a busy seaside holiday town, lies nearly 6 miles WNW from Watchet. Its small drying harbour, which can be crowded during the season, is formed by a single stone pier and is accessible about 2½ hr either side of HW. The best approach is from the NNW. The harbour is sheltered from N through W to SSE, but very exposed to the E. The sand and mud bottom slopes gently upwards from the entrance and keelboats can dry out on legs on the firmer inner part; ask the HM for directions before settling down. The town centre is a short walk from the harbour.

Tides HW Minehead is at HW Dover −4hr 50min, or HW Avonmouth −00hr 35min. Heights above datum are approximately: 10.8m MHWS, 0.9m MLWS, 8.2m MHWN, 3.5m MLWN.

Port Control The Harbour Master has his office on the inner part of the pier, tel (0843) 2566.

Tidal streams and currents

Streams off Minehead can be strong, reaching 4 or 5 knots at springs a mile offshore. The W-going stream begins 1¼ hr after local HW and runs for about 5 hr; the E-going stream begins soon after local LW and runs for nearly 7 hr.

Description

Although Minehead is a rather hectic resort, its small drying harbour is set back from the main rough and tumble of dubious seaside delights and is a congenial place to lie for a night. Bilge-keelers, centreboarders or keelboats with legs may all take the ground on the firm bottom, although boats using legs are better off in the inner part of the harbour on firmer sand. A substantial stone pier curves E and SE to provide good shelter from N through W to SSE. However, Minehead is very exposed to the E and it is unwise to enter

Minehead Harbour at half-tide, when there is usually enough water for shallow draught boats to reach the pierhead steps.

in easterly winds or to dry out there if easterlies are forecast.

At the end of the pier, on the inside, are the landing steps used by the numerous tripper, day-fishing and hire launches which provide plenty of activity for the visitor with time to sit and watch. These boats operate so long as there is enough water at the steps—normally anytime above half-tide for $2\frac{1}{2}$ ft draft. Most boats can enter the harbour 2 hr either side of HW, although those with more than $4\frac{1}{2}$ ft draft should wait until near HW.

On the quayside are a hotel, one or two cafes and a water tap near the HM's office. The town centre, with plenty of shops and a garage for fuel, is 10 minutes' walk from the harbour. The town is usually over-populated during the summer, being swamped periodically by the nearby Butlins campers.

Outer approaches

Coming from the E, either pass Warren Point a good mile off, to avoid the rocky drying ridge which extends well to seaward, or pass the point above half-tide when the ridge is safe to cross. Give shallow Minehead Bay a similar offing (Butlins holiday camp is conspicuous at the head of the bay) and aim to approach the harbour from $\frac{3}{4}$ mile NNW of the pierhead. There is a white mark low down on the cliff abreast this 'fairway' position. If the tide is too low to enter Minehead anchor near the white mark about 2 cables offshore in $3\frac{1}{2}$m, i.e. roughly midway between Greenaleigh Point and the beacon off Minehead which stands on the base of the old pier.

Coming from the W is straightforward, but pass Foreland Point at least $1\frac{1}{2}$ miles off to avoid the worst of its overfalls. If there is not enough rise of tide to enter Minehead anchor about $\frac{1}{2}$ mile ESE of Greenaleigh Point, abreast the white mark as above.

Entry

Only approach Minehead within 2 hr of HW, sounding carefully on the way in. From the fairway position $\frac{3}{4}$ mile NNW of the pierhead, i.e. $\frac{1}{2}$ mile to seaward of the white mark, bring the pierhead into transit with Conygar Tower (conspicuous about 2 miles SE of the harbour) on a bearing of 155°Mag. Follow the line, leaving the old pier beacon well to starboard, and round the pierhead 25m off.

Entry at night

Feasible for strangers in quiet weather and good visibility, although a paucity of navigation lights can make it tricky to gauge your distance off. Make for the fairway position by bringing Minehead pierhead light (2FG vert, 4M, vis 127°–262°T) onto a safe bearing of 155°Mag. while you are still a mile offshore. Then simply approach the pierhead along this line, sounding as you go.

Berths and anchorages

Minehead Harbour Go alongside the pier initially, well W of the landing steps, and ask the HM for directions. The inner part of the harbour is firm enough to dry out on legs.

Anchorage outside the harbour The waiting anchorage between Greenaleigh Point and the old pier beacon is sheltered from due W through S to SSE. On neap tides shoal-draft boats can fetch up E of the white mark, further towards Minehead and outside the old pier beacon.

Porlock Weir

Summary This fascinating miniature harbour lies in the SW corner of Porlock Bay, 6 miles W from Minehead and a similar distance ESE from Foreland Point. The tiny 'dock' is entered 1–1½ hr either side of HW via a short channel and a pair of gates. The gates are usually left open and the harbour allowed to dry, but there is a firm bottom for taking the ground and a quay to lie alongside. The dock provides good shelter from all quarters, although fresh E or NE winds send in a swell near HW. Just outside the gates is a small pool retained by the shingle bar at the E end of the entrance channel, with about 3ft 6in at LW.

Tides HW at Porlock Weir is at HW Dover − 5hr 00min, or HW Avonmouth −00hr 45min. Heights above chart datum: 10.2m MHWS, 0.8m MLWS, 7.8m MHWN, 3.4m MLWN.

Port Control The Harbour Master's office is on the W side of the entrance gates, tel (064381) 523.

Tidal streams and currents

The streams are moderate in Porlock Bay, but stronger (up to 3½ knots) in the offing. When approaching Porlock Bay from the W, note that the stream can reach 4–5 knots off Foreland Point, where heavy overfalls often extend over a mile offshore.

Description

Porlock Bay's shingle foreshore represents the first sign, as you work W along

Approaches to Porlock Weir

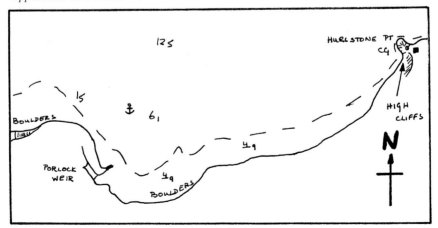

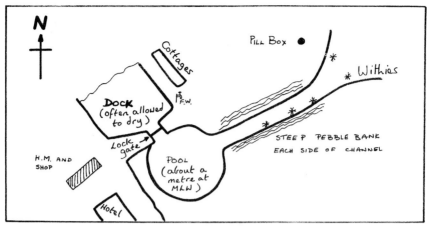

Porlock Weir

the English side of the Bristol Channel, that this cruising ground is not composed entirely of drying sand and mud. As you round Hurlstone Point from the E, the coast begins to undergo a subtle but discernible change. It will soon become higher, more rugged and generally steep-to, the elusive shoals of the upper reaches giving way to hard, tangible rock; the tides will still be fast, but not so savage as further up-Channel.

Porlock Weir, tucked into the corner of Porlock Bay, is a delightfully salty little haven. From the shelter of the tiny drying dock you can hear the sea breaking on the beach outside. The weather-worn thatched cottages look as though they've withstood generations of both occupants and winter gales. The Anchor Hotel is a seasoned nautical hostelry where local pilots used to pass the time of day and wait for business.

Porlock Weir makes an interesting port of call in quiet conditions, or in any winds from W through S to SE. The narrow entrance channel leads between shingle banks to a small pool where up to a dozen shoal-draft boats can lie afloat. On the NW side of this pool a pair of gates gives access to the dock area. They are usually left open and so the dock dries at about half-tide. However, you can safely take the ground on legs, or alongside a stone quay on the W side of the harbour.

Approach and entry

It is not advisable to approach Porlock Weir in even moderate E or NE winds. Both the entrance and the anchorage are very exposed from this quarter and Hurlstone Point offers practically no shelter, even in true easterlies.

Coming from the E, the approach is straightforward: round Hurlstone Point and make for the hotel and cottages in the SW corner of Porlock Bay.

Coming from the W, clear Foreland Point by a good 1½ miles to avoid the worst of its overfalls. Just W of Porlock Bay, avoid the drying spit which extends about 2 cables NW from Gore Point.

In quiet weather, if early on the tide, you can anchor over a patch of sand abreast the line of thatched cottages, just N of Porlock Weir entrance channel. Don't leave this anchorage until 1½ hr before HW, but then enter between the two tallest withies at the E end of the channel. Leave all other withies close to port as you pass between the shingle banks to the pool.

If you draw less than about 3½ ft you can stay afloat in the pool, if there is room. Otherwise carry on through the gates into the dock area. You may have to put someone ashore first to ask the Harbour Master to roll the footbridge aside.

Entry at night

Not recommended since the entrance is unlit. Foreland Point is the nearest light (Fl4, 15s), 6 miles to the W. But in settled offshore weather and good visibility, it is possible to sound carefully into Porlock Bay and anchor— provided you are sure of your position before closing the coast. The lights of the Anchor Hotel can sometimes help you in.

Berths and anchorages

Porlock Weir Boats drawing less than 3½ft can stay afloat in the small pool just outside the entrance gates. It is best to moor bow to the beach with an anchor out astern. This attractive spot is well sheltered except from the E and NE, but can be crowded during the season.

The entrance to Porlock Weir inner dock. The gates are usually left open so that yachts inside dry out on firm sand and shingle.

Opposite:
The narrow entrance channel into Porlock Weir, looking ENE towards Hurlstone Point.

The inner dock at Porlock Weir, looking towards the entrance gate and the Anchor Hotel. There is good shelter in the dock and you dry out on a firm sand and shingle bottom.

Porlock Weir dock You can pass through the gates into the dock and dry out on a firm bottom. Keelboats either lie alongside the W quay, or rig legs and anchor fore-and-aft. Inside the dock you are well protected from all quarters, and handy for Porlock Weir's two hotels and general store. There is a garage at Porlock village, about 20 minutes' walk inland.

Anchorage in Porlock Bay The holding is generally very poor because of the coarse shingle bottom. However, the sandy patch just off the line of thatched cottages offers a reasonable anchorage in quiet weather. It is prudent to lie to two heavy anchors if staying overnight.

Foreland Point

This gaunt headland juts into the Channel 6 miles W from Porlock Bay. Foreland Ledge, a narrow rocky bank 2 miles long, lies between ½ and 1 mile N of the Foreland. The combination of headland, ledge and strong tides often produces heavy overfalls over a mile offshore, particularly on the ebb with the wind in the W. It is therefore advisable to clear Foreland Point by at least 1½ miles. Foreland Ledge has a least depth of 6.9m.

Close W of Foreland Point is Sand Ridge, a narrow shoal about a mile long whose E tip dries 0.3m. The W end of Sand Ridge is marked by a green conical buoy (unlit), moored 1.6 miles W by N from Foreland Point. There is a narrow passage 2 cables wide between the drying part of Sand Ridge and the Foreland, but it is usually best to pass at least a mile to seaward of Sand Ridge buoy.

Lynmouth

Lynmouth Bay curves westward from Foreland Point, and the shallow River Lyn flows into its SW part across an uneven shelf of drying rocks and boulders. Lynton village lies on the W side of the river and Lynmouth on the E side. Lynton has a small drying pier harbour with about $4\frac{1}{2}$m at MHWS. A few local boats are based here, but its tricky approach is not recommended to strangers. There is a 'lunchtime' anchorage in Lynmouth Bay in quiet weather, but the high ground between Foreland Point and Hollerday Hill has a rather menacing character, and I wouldn't linger too long.

Combe Martin

This small coastal village is 10 miles W from Foreland Point and about 3 miles E from Ilfracombe. There is a useful passage anchorage off Combe Martin, sheltered from any wind with S in it. In quiet conditions you can land by dinghy at a quay near the village, although the small harbour area is susceptible to swell and not suitable for taking the ground. Anchor as far into the bay as depth and draft allow, but watch out for the drying rocky ledges which extend seawards from either side of the entrance to the inlet leading to the village.

Pilotage into Combe Martin is straightforward. Come directly in from seaward, but make the final approach towards the village from the NW, giving a wide berth to the point on the N side. Keep an eye on the echo-sounder as you draw into the bay. Copperas Rock with 2.4m over it lies just over $1\frac{1}{2}$ miles ENE of the outer anchorage, marked on its seaward side by Copperas green conical buoy (unlit). Except for the two pierhead lights shown from Lynmouth's tricky drying harbour (2FR vert and 2FG vert), there are no navigation lights along this stretch of coast between Foreland Point (Fl4, 15s, 26M) and Ilfracombe's Lantern Hill (FR, 6M).

Watermouth

Summary The narrow inlet known as Watermouth Cove lies a mile W of Combe Martin and a similar distance E of Ilfracombe. Hemmed in by high cliffs, this attractive natural haven is entered between Widmouth Head and

Combe Martin to Foreland Point

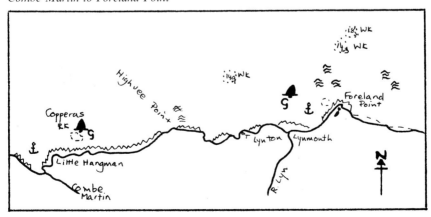

Burrow Nose. There is often broken water off the entrance, especially on a weather-going ebb, and the cross-tide can be powerful. Once inside there is good shelter in all but strong N through NW winds. Even then, a low breakwater in the cove affords fair protection. Watermouth mostly dries, but you can settle down on a firm bottom. At neaps boats of moderate draft can stay afloat in the outer part.

Tides HW Watermouth is at HW Dover − 5hr 20min, or HW Milford Haven − 00hr 10min. Heights above chart datum: 9.2m MHWS, 0.7m MLWS, 6.9m MHWN, 3.0m MLWN.

Port Control Watermouth and its moorings are administered privately and visitors should report their arrival to the chandlery at the head of the cove.

Tidal streams and currents

The streams can be strong off the entrance, up to $3\frac{1}{2}$ knots at springs, and a weather-going tide often causes broken water. The E-going stream begins about 1 hr after local LW, and the W-going stream about 1 hr after local HW.

Description

Just over a mile E of Ilfracombe, Watermouth Cove is a rather picturesque natural inlet about $\frac{1}{4}$ mile long, entered between the high cliffs of Widmouth Head to the W and a lower promontory known as Burrow Nose to the E. It practically dries at LAT to a firm bottom of sand and shale, but makes a quiet and pleasant overnight stop for boats which can take the ground easily. There is good shelter in all but strong N through NW winds; even under these conditions a half-tide breakwater, which partly divides the inlet, helps provide a fair degree of protection. This breakwater is marked by two yellow spar beacons and has a green spar beacon at its NE end. There is a tide gauge close SE of the green beacon.

At the head of the cove is a small quay, a couple of landing slips, a chandlery shop and the Watermouth Yacht Club. The Harbour Master can usually be

Watermouth Cove

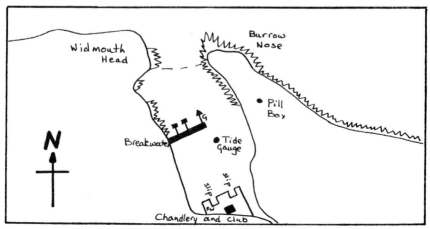

Watermouth Cove, looking WNW towards the entrance. You can see the low, half-tide breakwater, which helps protect the inner part of the inlet from any swell which finds its way in.

found in the chandlery; the company which runs this shop also administers the moorings in Watermouth and owns the nearby caravan site. Visitors arriving out of hours should enter their details on the visiting craft noticeboard near the chandlery. Mooring fees should be paid to the HM or the reception office near the site entrance.

Approach and entry

The entrance to Watermouth can be difficult to identify from offshore; it is a little way E of the Coastguard cottages on Rillage Point. There is also a small ruined pillbox on Burrow Nose not far E of the entrance. Strangers should only approach Watermouth within 2 hr of HW. There are often boisterous overfalls outside the mouth of the cove during the strongest part of the tide, but the entrance between Widmouth Head and Burrow Nose is clear of dangers. Be prepared to allow for a powerful cross-set when lining up to come in. Entering under sail can be tricky because of the unpredictable down-draughts from Widmouth Head. Once into the inlet turn SE towards the head of the cove and sound carefully as you go.

Entry at night

Do not attempt to enter at night.

Berths and anchorages

At neaps, shoal-draft boats can lie afloat at anchor in the outer part of the cove. For the best shelter tuck inside the half-tide breakwater, leaving the green spar beacon to starboard. Keelboats can dry out safely on legs provided there is no swell. There are a few visitors' moorings, which have red buoys with yellow handles. If you use one of these report your arrival to the HM as soon as possible. Watermouth YC welcomes visitors.

Ilfracombe

Summary Ilfracombe harbour lies 12 miles W along the coast from Foreland Point and 3½ miles E from Bull Point. It is often used as a staging-post by yachts, being one of the safest and most accessible havens on the S shore of the Bristol Channel. It is completely sheltered from the W and makes a good port of refuge in SW gales. The inner harbour dries and is protected from the E by a breakwater; it can be entered 2–3 hr either side of HW, depending on draft. The outer anchorage can be entered at any state of tide and offers good shelter except from between N and ENE. The attractive town has all facilities and Ilfracombe YC welcomes visitors.

Tides HW Ilfracombe is at HW Dover − 5hr 25min, or HW Milford Haven − 00hr 15min. Heights above chart datum: 9.2m MHWS, 0.7m MLWS, 6.9m MHWN, 3.0m MLWN.

Port Control The Harbour Master's office is on the N side of the inner harbour, tel (0271) 63969.

Tidal streams and currents

Streams can reach 3½ knots off the entrance at springs, and there may be overfalls up to ½ mile W of Rillage Point especially on the ebb. The E-going stream begins about an hour after local LW, and the W-going stream about 1 hr after local HW.

Description

Huddled behind Compass and Lantern Hills, Ilfracombe's attractive half-tide inner harbour probably offers the best shelter on the S shore of the Bristol

The attractive and well sheltered inner harbour at Ilfracombe, with conspicuous Lantern Hill and its old chapel in the background.

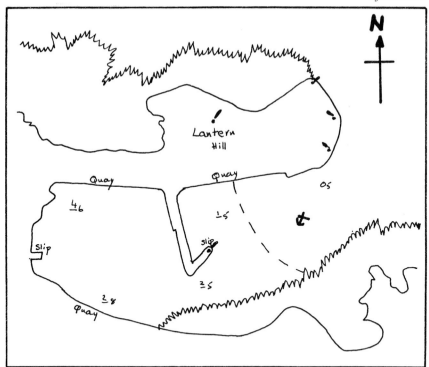

Ilfracombe

Channel. It is accessible for 2–3 hr either side of HW, but you can always get some way into the outer bay except at dead low springs. This outer harbour area is entered just over a cable to the E of Lantern Hill, and is well protected from the S and W but rather exposed to the NE. It is used regularly by the Lundy Island supply ship which berths alongside the Promenade Pier near HW.

Ilfracombe has a good selection of shops and is busy during the holiday season, but not so frantic as the larger resorts of Minehead and Weston further up-Channel. There are useful facilities for yachts, including chandlers, marine engineers, not to mention the bar and showers at the hospitable Ilfracombe Yacht Club. The club premises are on the first floor above the Harbour Master's office, on the N quay of the inner harbour. The HM is always very helpful to visitors.

Approach and entry

Coming from the W, pass well outside Morte Stone green conical buoy (unlit) to avoid Morte Stone itself and Rockham shoal. In quiet conditions you can cut within ½ mile of Bull Point to dodge the worst of the race. In heavy weather avoid the race altogether by passing N of Horseshoe Rocks N-cardinal buoy. If arriving on the W-going tide, you can sometimes catch a favourable eddy by keeping close inshore between Bull Point and Lantern Hill.

Coming from the E, pass outside Copperas Rock green conical buoy (unlit) and then steer W by S to round Widmouth Head and Rillage Point. There can be overfalls up to ½ mile W of Rillage Point, especially during the middle hours of the ebb.

Ilfracombe outer harbour is entered not quite 1½ cables E of Lantern Hill, recognised by the small chapel on its summit, and immediately E of Promenade Pier. Keep towards the pier as you come in, to avoid the drying ledges which fringe the S part of the bay. Have the echo-sounder running and anchor on a line ENE of the breakwater head as far in as depth allows. There is a least depth of about 1½m in the outer harbour 2 hr after MLWS. The inner harbour can be entered from 2–3 hr either side of HW depending on draft.

Entry at night

Coming from the W, first pick up Bull Point light (Fl3, 10s, 25M, and FR 058°–096°T), 3½ miles W of Ilfracombe. The flashing light is obscured from inside Barnstaple Bay and the fixed red shines towards Lundy Island. Horseshoe N-cardinal buoy is lit (QW), 3 miles due N Mag. from Bull Point. As you approach Ilfracombe, pick up Lantern Hill light (FR, 6M) close W of the entrance.

From the E, the last navigation light before Ilfracombe is 12 miles away at Foreland Point (Fl4, 15s, 26M). Keep well offshore until you can identify Lantern Hill light (FR, 6M) as above.

Final approach: when entering at night, come in from due N to a position 1½ cables E of Lantern Hill light. Then head WSW towards the inner pierhead (2FG, vert), leaving Promenade Pier close to starboard. During the winter (1 Sept to 30 April) Promenade Pier shows three pairs of fixed green vertical lights.

Berths and anchorages

Ilfracombe Outer Harbour There is a least depth of 1.8m off Promenade Pier and then the bottom shoals gradually to dry 1.5m just E of the breakwater. Edge in after LW, keeping an eye on the echo-sounder. Fetch up well away from Promenade Pier and clear of the fairway leading to the inner harbour; remember that some of the local boats will be able to move before you can. It is best to anchor fore-and-aft if staying in the outer harbour overnight.

Ilfracombe Inner Harbour Dries to a firm sandy bottom. Enter as soon after half-tide as draft permits. The fairway dries to 2.5m just S of the inner pierhead, so deeper draft yachts should delay entry until 2 hr before HW. Go alongside the S quay initially and ask the HM about a berth. There are a few visitors' moorings in the harbour or you can dry out alongside one of the quays. Do not moor so as to obstruct the lifeboat slip. Fresh water can be obtained from a tap on the breakwater.

Passage-making from Ilfracombe

If you are bound well down-Channel from Ilfracombe, aim to leave about an hour before local HW. You'll push some foul tide for an hour or so, but the stream will be easing as you come up with Bull Point. There are two advantages in this. The overfalls which can extend up to 3 miles N from Bull Point should be settling down; and you will also have arrived at an important milestone along this coast with the tide about to turn in your favour, carry you nicely round Hartland Point and set you well on your way down the North Cornwall coast. The streams are much weaker beyond Hartland and it is quite feasible to press on against the new flood.

If you are bound round the corner for Appledore and the River Torridge, leave Ilfracombe about ½ hr before local LW. This means coming out of the inner harbour in good time and anchoring in the outer harbour in plenty of water. Outside Ilfracombe you will have a fair tide for a while, but the stream will be falling slack off Bull Point and the race with it. You should have slack water round Morte Point and Baggy Point, and once you are well into Barnstaple Bay the tides are much weaker anyway. You must not cross Bideford Bar until about 2½ hr before the next HW so you may have some time to kill in Barnstaple Bay.

If bound well up-Channel from Ilfracombe, leave an hour before local LW, push the last of the foul tide and then pick up nearly 7 hr of the new flood.

Appledore, Instow and Bideford

Summary The Taw and Torridge estuary opens into the E side of Barnstaple Bay, 3½ miles S of Baggy Point and 11 miles ENE of Hartland Point. Entry involves crossing Bideford Bar, which can be dangerous in heavy onshore weather. A buoyed channel leads to the small shipbuilding town of Appledore. Instow lies opposite Appledore on the E bank of the Torridge, and Bideford is only 2 miles upstream. There are plans for a marina at Knapp Lands, just above Appledore on the W bank. The River Taw joins the estuary N of Instow and shoal-draft boats with local knowledge can reach Barnstaple, 5 miles up, near HWS.

Tides HW at Appledore or Bideford is at HW Dover − 5hr 25min. Heights above chart datum at Appledore: 7.5m MHWS, 0.2m MLWS, 5.2m MHWN, 1.6m MLWN. HW Barnstaple is about 15min later than HW Appledore.

Port Control For local advice call Appledore Pilots within 2 hr of HW on VHF Ch 16, working Ch 6, 9 or 12.

Tidal streams and currents

Although tides in the outer approaches can be strong (up to 3 knots at springs off both Hartland Point and Morte Point), they are considerably weaker in Barnstaple Bay. A hard current runs in the lower Torridge through Appledore Pool, especially near half-ebb.

Description

The wide estuary of the Taw and Torridge Rivers flows into Barnstaple Bay between the low-lying dunes known as Braunton Burrows to the N, and Grey's Hill and Appledore town to the S. The buoyed entrance channel is accessible in moderate conditions for about 2½ hr either side of HW; it leads across Bideford Bar and then between extensive sandbanks to Appledore Pool. Appledore is a small but busy seafaring town which includes

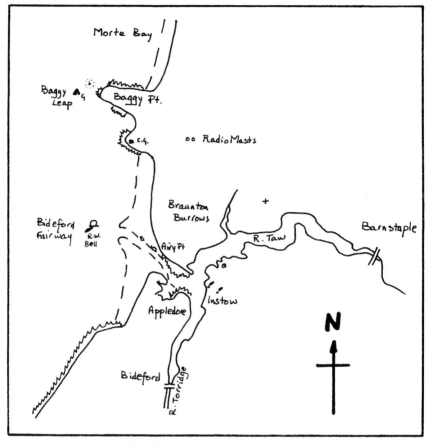

Approaches to the Torridge Estuary

shipbuilding among its activities. Coasters call here regularly, which is why the buoyage is so well maintained.

Instow lies opposite Appledore on the E bank of the river, a quiet seaside village with broad drying sands, a useful quay and the attractively situated North Devon Yacht Club. Visitors are welcome at the club and there is plenty of room for shoal-draft boats to dry out. From Instow, a picturesque 2 mile trip up the Torridge brings you to the old market town of Bideford, where the stone arches of the road-bridge call an effective halt to navigation. On the W bank, visitors can take the mud alongside the quay but should check with the HM before settling down.

The Taw joins the estuary a little way N of Instow, a much shallower and more tortuous river than the Torridge. Although the interesting town of Barnstaple lies only 5 miles upstream, strangers are advised not to attempt the passage without reliable local knowledge.

Outer approaches

Coming down-Channel, aim to arrive off Bull Point near slack water low, when the overfalls should be fairly quiet. Morte Point is $1\frac{1}{2}$ miles WSW of Bull Point and the shore between the two is patchy with off-lying rocks. Avoid

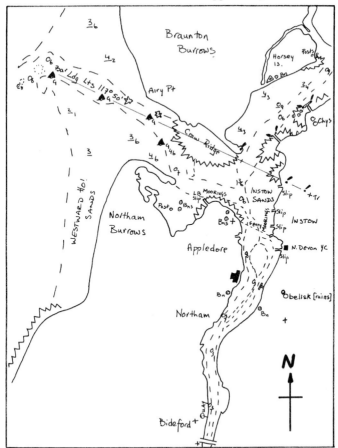

The Torridge Estuary

Rockham Shoal ½ mile NE of Morte Point, and pass outside Morte Stone green conical buoy (unlit) which marks the ledge extending W from Morte Point.

The coast now trends S into Barnstaple Bay, past sandy Morte Bay and the high, imposing promontory of Baggy Point. Baggy Rock lurks 4 cables W by N of this headland, marked by Baggy Leap green conical buoy (unlit). From Baggy Leap make good due S Mag. for 3½ miles to locate Bideford Fairway buoy (LFl, 10s, RWVS, bell). If you were off Bull Head at slack water low, you will probably arrive off Bideford Fairway too early; don't venture further inshore from here until 2½ hr before HW. In quiet weather you can anchor ½ mile W of the buoy in about 13m, sand and mud. In any winds S of W there is a useful anchorage in Clovelly Bay, nearly 7 miles SW of the Fairway buoy in about 7m over mud.

Coming up-Channel, the race off Hartland Point is the main danger. In quiet weather pass about ¾ mile off the headland and inside the worst of the overfalls. Otherwise stay 3–4 miles off, outside the race. When bound for Appledore it is preferable to round Hartland near slack water low, but you will then have to anchor or jill about off the Fairway buoy until 2½ hr before HW.

Entry

Do not try to enter the Torridge estuary in poor visibility or in fresh onshore winds. Otherwise, leave Bideford Fairway buoy 2 cables to starboard and then make good 125°Mag. for just over a mile to pick up the 'Bar' buoy (unlit but with fluorescent paint panels); this is the first of four green conical buoys which indicate the channel as far as Appledore. There is a pair of leading marks on the shore just N of Instow, but they are difficult to identify from seaward in daylight. It is better to steer a careful course between the buoys, since the Fairway and the first three green conical buoys all lie close S of the straight line 125°Mag. which is the bearing of the leading marks in transit.

Leave the Bar buoy close to starboard and continue to make good 125°Mag. for just over another mile, leaving Middle Ridge (unlit) and Outer Pulley (QFlG) green conicals to starboard. Then come onto 167°Mag. and steer for the Inner Pulley green conical buoy (unlit). Leave this close to starboard and stay on 167°Mag. towards the SE tip of the line of dunes known as Grey Sand Hills. Come to port off this low point, steering about 110°Mag. towards Appledore Pool. The Appledore lifeboat may be moored off her slip, and you can fetch up just below the lifeboat or further upstream beyond two other large mooring buoys (see below).

Entry at night

Not recommended for strangers, but Bideford Fairway buoy is lit (LFl, 10s) and Instow leading lights (Front Occ 6s, Rear Occ 10s) take you as far in as the Outer Pulley buoy (QFlG).

Berths and anchorages

Appledore Pool Keelboats can anchor and stay afloat in the pool between Grey Sand Hills and Instow Sands. The tide can run strongly through this area especially near half-ebb and there is better holding at the E end, upstream from the large mooring buoys. Be sure to tripline your anchor as there are numerous old cables on the bottom. Land at Appledore Quay, where there is a water tap. Shops are nearby in the town.

Appledore Quay Carry on above the pool, turn S into the River Torridge and round up alongside Appledore Quay. Keelboats can take the ground here, but check with the HM before you dry out (tel Bideford (02372) 4569). The quay can be difficult for bilge-keelers in certain places where the bottom slopes outwards.

Mouth of the River Taw Appledore Pool can be uncomfortable in fresh winds from between N and WNW. Then you can tuck a little way into the River Taw and anchor in 1.8m with Crow Point lighthouse (FlR, 5s) bearing WSW distant 1½ cables. There is moderate holding here in fine sand, and this position is about as far into the Taw as you can go without grounding at LW.

Instow In reasonable weather bilge-keelers can dry out on the S part of Instow Sands or in the shoal area opposite Instow Quay. You can either anchor or use a vacant mooring by arrangement with the North Devon YC. Instow Quay can be reached when the height of tide is more than about 4.6m, and keelboats can take the ground alongside by arrangement with the club. Shops are handy

The town quay at Bideford, with the quaint stone arches of the old bridge in the background.

at Instow village and there is fresh water at the quay.

The River Torridge There are various drying anchorages between Appledore and Bideford. Northam is a sheltered and attractive spot $\frac{1}{2}$ mile above Appledore shipyard on the W side of the river.

Bideford Quay To reach Bideford, leave Appledore 2 hr before HW and keep broadly to the W side of the river. Yachts can moor alongside the town quay by arrangement with the Harbour Master, whose office is in the square (tel Bideford (02372) 2321). It is important to check with the HM before drying out, because in some places the bottom slopes outwards and in others the mud is very soft. The town is nearby and there is fresh water at the quay.

Clovelly

The town huddles under the shelter of some rather forbidding high ground in the SW corner of Barnstaple Bay, about 7 miles SW of Bideford Fairway buoy and 5 miles ESE of Hartland Point. A stone pier curves round to the SE to protect the tiny drying harbour from seaward, but prolonged onshore winds are liable to send a swell into Barnstaple Bay and make it inadvisable to enter Clovelly. In offshore winds, from between SW through S to SE, there is a useful anchorage a little way ESE of the harbour entrance. This can be a good place to wait for sufficient rise of tide if you are bound for the Torridge estuary.

The approach to Clovelly is best made from the NE near HW, and strangers should negotiate the entrance with caution. Over the years a steep pebble ridge has built across from the shore side, restricting safe access to boats with about a $4\frac{1}{2}$ft draft. If in doubt about going in, anchor outside and either seek local advice or take soundings from the dinghy. The deepest water lies close to the

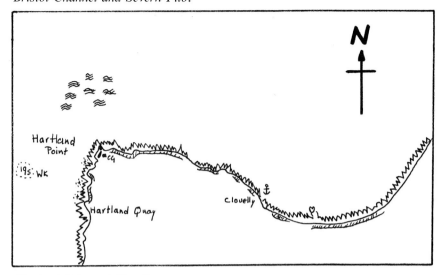

Hartland Point and Clovelly

pierhead. In calm settled weather yachts can dry out on firm sandy mud alongside the inner wall of the pier.

There are limited supplies in the village and fresh water is usually obtainable by can from the lifeboat house on the beach. The Harbour Master, who runs one of the pleasure boats, will be able to help with any problems or enquiries.

Lundy Island

The windswept granite plateau of Lundy Island lies 10 miles NW of Hartland Point, out in the main streams of the Bristol Channel. Owned by the National Trust, Lundy is maintained as a bird sanctuary and is worth a visit in settled weather. There are some interesting historic sites, among them the ruins of the 13th century Marisco Castle.

Not quite 3 miles from N to S and little more than ½ mile across, Lundy is high, steep-to, and surrounded by tidal races and overfalls. Strangers should only approach in quiet conditions near slack water. The usual anchorage in westerlies is off the SE landing beach, just to the N of Rat Island and the S lighthouse; edge in as close as your draft permits and fetch up in 5–9m. The cliffs provide good shelter here in any winds from between NW and SSW, even in gales, but the anchorage is exposed to the E. Be sure to veer sufficient cable to allow for the considerable rise of tide, and keep well clear of the heavy wire which runs into the sea for the use of local supply boats.

If there is any E in the wind you can anchor on the W side of Lundy at Jenny's Cove, provided there is no swell. There is a good walk to the top of the cliff path, with spectacular views back across to Hartland Point and the Devon coast.

Although Lundy has strong tides, no harbour and rather uneasy waters, it is nevertheless fascinating to sail out to the island for a day, starting from Appledore or Ilfracombe. It is best to choose a period when the tides are about

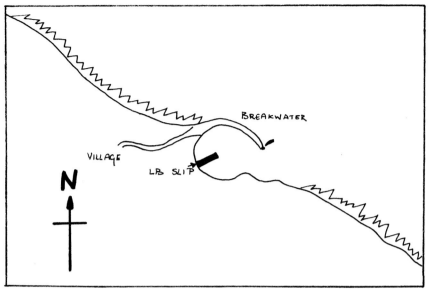

Clovelly harbour

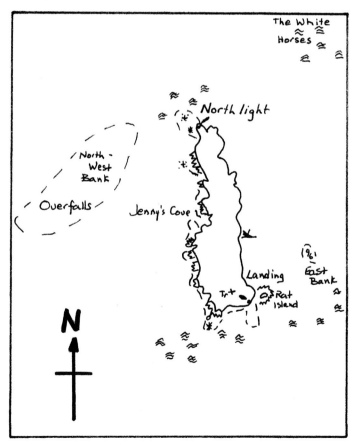

Lundy Island

halfway between springs and neaps, and taking off; you will then have a convenient morning and evening HW, a fairish stream to Lundy and back, and overfalls that are not too savage.

Provisions are available at the local stores and refreshment at the hospitable Marisco Tavern.

At night

Strangers are advised not to approach Lundy at night, but the two powerful lights at either end of the island are important marks for navigators in the vicinity: Lundy North Light (Fl2, 20s, 24M); Lundy South Light (Fl5s, 24M). South lighthouse has an RDF beacon (296.5 kHz, **LS**, 50M, No. 3).

Bude

Summary Bude Haven lies 11 miles S of Hartland Point and its outer part is no more than a narrow drying channel on the W side of a shallow river estuary. A long Atlantic swell often breaks over the outer shoals and strangers should only enter in quiet weather, during daylight and near HW. A few local moorings are protected from the W by a breakwater which runs out from the shore to Chapel Rock. The Bude Canal joins the sea in the S part of the estuary and yachts can lock in when the height of tide is more than 5½m. Given calm conditions the approaches to Bude are straightforward, with two sets of leading marks indicating the deepest water.

Tides HW Bude is at HW Dover − 5hr 40min, or HW Milford Haven − 00hr 40min. HW heights above chart datum: 7.7m MHWS and 5.8m MHWN. There are no published LW heights.

Port Control North Cornwall District Council, HM Peter Cloke, tel Bude (0288) 3111. Call 'Bude Harbour Office' on VHF Ch 16, working on Ch 12.

Tidal streams and currents

Once you have 'turned the corner' and are well S of Hartland Point, you avoid the main, powerful flow of the Bristol Channel. The streams therefore tend to be weak along the N Cornish coast.

Description

Bude, a small and friendly Cornish seaside town, is the first haven that you come across on the way S from Hartland Point. Although the coast in the vicinity of Hartland is high, Bude itself is low-lying. The harbour consists of the comparatively sheltered W side of a shallow river estuary, which faces NW and dries out to firm sand. The narrow river channel where the local moorings are laid is protected by a breakwater built between the shore and off-lying Chapel Rock.

There is usually a long Atlantic swell rolling in from seaward, which breaks over the outer shoals on the N side of the estuary. The approach to Bude Haven is made from the SW, leaving these breakers to port and Chapel Rock to starboard. Moderate onshore winds from between W and NNW will considerably increase the extent of the breaking seas and so strangers are advised only to enter Bude in quiet weather or offshore winds.

The old Bude Canal connects with the sea by way of a tidal lock about $\frac{1}{2}$ mile SE of Chapel Rock. This peaceful waterway was built in 1826 to carry shell sand inland to improve the acid soil. Now, the lower stretch below the road-bridge makes a peaceful basin for a few yachts and fishing boats. Visitors are recommended to lock into the canal and entry is normally restricted to 2 hr either side of HW. Bude's well served town centre is not far from the canal quay.

Approach and entry

The outer approaches to Bude are clear of dangers and the passages S from Hartland and NE from Padstow are both straightforward. In W winds, though, a good offing should be kept from this rather craggy and unforgiving lee shore.

Conspicuous from the N or from seaward are the large radar dish aerials at Lower Sharpnose Point. Even from the SW, these aerials are often the most obvious landmarks. The entrance to Bude lies 3 miles S along the coast from Lower Sharpnose Point.

Compass Point, a little way S of Bude entrance, can be identified by a

Bude Haven

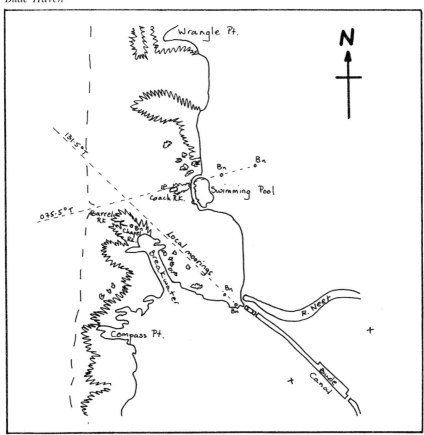

prominent tower with a flagstaff on its N side. The final approach to Bude is from the SW, and you should first make for a position about 6 cables NW of Compass Point. From here, pick up the outer set of leading marks which are above the low cliffs on the N side of the estuary. The front outer mark is a white spar with a yellow diamond topmark, and the rear outer mark is a white flagstaff. These two in transit bearing 082°Mag. leave a green barrel beacon at the end of the breakwater close to starboard.

Once past this beacon, turn to starboard towards the SE and bring the inner set of leading marks to bear; these are located ½ cable W of the canal lock. The front inner mark is a white pile beacon and the rear inner mark a white spar, both with yellow triangular topmarks. These two in transit bearing 138°Mag. take you up to the lock entrance. There is a small quay just outside the lock, marked at its seaward end by a green spar beacon. The lock can only be worked when the tide is 5.5m above datum. Inside the canal yachts can moor on the N bank to bollards and rings.

The best time to enter or leave Bude is between HW and HW $+\frac{1}{2}$hr, when the incoming surge will have lost its momentum. Follow both sets of leading marks carefully and don't be tempted to come straight in from seaward onto the second pair. Strangers should not approach Bude if a heavy ground swell is running, when in any case the lock may not be able to operate. In calm weather there is usually sufficient depth to enter or leave within 2 hr of HW, but always keep an eye on the echo-sounder. If possible give the Harbour Master 24 hours' advance notice of your ETA.

Entry at night

This is not recommended and no lights are shown.

The sheltered berths in the old Bude Canal, looking towards the entrance. Visitors should lie alongside the north quay, moored to bollards or rings.

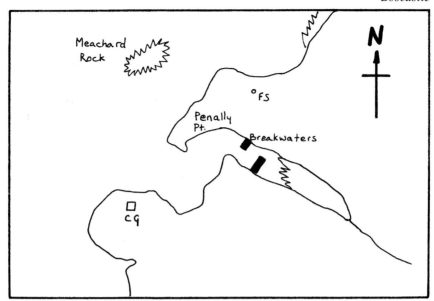

Meachard
Rock

° FS

Penally
Pt.

Breakwaters

□
CG

Boscastle

Berths and anchorages

Bude Canal Although it is expensive to lock in and out, the canal provides the only safe berth for visitors and is quiet, sheltered and handy for the town. Fresh water is available from the inshore lifeboat house at the lock gates and also on the canal quay. Diesel and petrol by can from the local garage.

Boscastle

This tiny harbour lies 10 miles SSW from Bude. Almost invisible from seaward, it is entered via a narrow dogleg gully hewn out of natural rock. The inner part is protected by two short breakwaters. Now owned by the National Trust, Boscastle was built by Sir Richard Grenville in 1584 and was Launceston's main port for shipping slate and corn, as well as importing coal.

Only approach Boscastle in quiet weather, during daylight and near HW. The entrance can be difficult to identify but Meachard Rock is the key mark, 37m high and 1½ cables offshore. A Coastguard hut stands on the S arm of the entrance and there is a flagstaff on the hill above Penally Point, which forms the N arm.

Pass outside Meachard and steer for the white Coastguard hut until the harbour opens up between the cliffs to port. Then head straight in, keeping to mid-channel. Leave the outer breakwater to port and come to starboard round the inner breakwater. Don't go too far into the harbour, where it is rocky and unsuitable for drying out, but stay close to the inner mole where the bottom is stony sand and mud. It is best to moor bow to the quay like the local fishing boats, with an anchor out astern. Watch out for the onset of any swell, which can set you bumping as you dry.

The village is attractive, although busy with tourists during the season. Fresh water is obtainable at the head of the harbour.

The amazing little harbour at Boscastle is hemmed-in by cliffs and practically invisible from seaward. The only practical berths are in the west corner, just inside the inner breakwater near the local fishing boats. Moor bows to the quay with a buoyed anchor out astern.

Port Isaac harbour dries at half-tide and is subject to swell in onshore winds. Visitors should seek the advice of the Harbour Master before committing themselves to taking the ground.

Port Isaac

The entrance to this picturesque drying harbour lies $\frac{1}{2}$ mile ESE of Varley Head and 5 miles roughly SSW of Tintagel Head. Port Isaac can be located from seaward by steering S by E towards St Endellion church tower, conspicuous a little way inland. When entering, keep over towards Lobber Point and make for the head of the W breakwater to avoid Kenwal and Warrant Rocks, two drying ledges lurking due N of the E breakwater.

Port Isaac faces due N and dries to firm sand at about half-tide. There is very little shelter in onshore winds, when a nasty surge can find its way into the harbour. It is a good idea to take local advice before committing yourself to drying out. Moor stern-to the beach with an anchor out ahead, but keep well clear of local fishing boats. Port Isaac has some shops and a couple of pubs, and is a very pleasant spot in any winds from the S.

Do not attempt to enter the harbour at night. The whole of this stretch of coast is unlit between Stepper Point (LFl, 10s, 4M) and Hartland Point (Fl6, 15s, 25M), a distance of over 30 miles.

Port Gaverne

A narrow inlet $\frac{1}{2}$ mile E of Port Isaac, Port Gaverne dries to a stone and pebble bottom and is only suitable for small local boats. In offshore winds, however, it can provide a pleasant lunchtime anchorage near the top of the tide.

Padstow and the River Camel

Summary The mouth of the Camel River faces NW between Stepper and Pentire Points, about 4 miles ENE of Trevose Head. The broad sandflat known as Doom Bar extends across the entrance from the W side towards Trebetherick Point, leaving only a narrow channel at LWS. Strangers should

Port Isaac and Port Gaverne

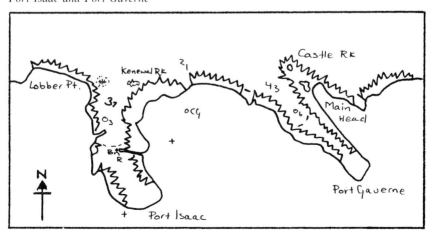

not enter until 2 hr before HW. The sea breaks heavily over the bar in strong winds from between N and NW. Padstow lies 1½ miles upstream from Doom Bar on the W bank. The harbour, which dries to mud, offers the best shelter on the N Cornish coast. Visiting yachts can take the ground alongside one of the quays close to the town. There is an anchorage outside the harbour in the Pool where moderate draft boats can stay afloat.

Tides HW Padstow is at HW Dover −05hr 55min or HW Milford Haven −00hr 50min. Heights above chart datum: 7.3m MHWS, 0.8m MLWS, 5.6m MHWN, 2.6m MLWN.

Port Control HM W. Lindsey. Call 'Padstow Harbour' on VHF Ch 16, working Ch 14, or telephone Padstow (0841) 532239.

Tidal streams and currents

The streams off Padstow are weak, generally less than a knot even at springs. In Padstow Bay the SW-going stream starts ¾ hr after local HW and the NE-going stream starts just before local LW.

Description

The River Camel has one of the most attractive and unspoilt estuaries in the West Country. The lower reaches are fringed with sandy beaches and the coastal approaches are not quite so forbidding as much of North Cornwall. The entrance, which is just over a mile wide, lies nearly 4 miles ENE of Trevose Head and faces NW between Stepper Point and Pentire Point. The main navigational danger is Doom Bar, a broad drying area of sand which extends

Approaches to Padstow

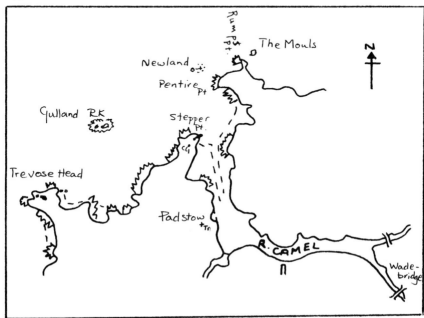

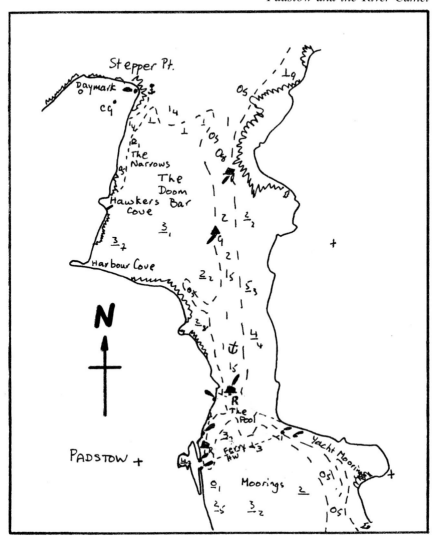

Padstow

almost right across the river from inside Stepper Point towards Trebetherick Point. Although the sea will break heavily over Doom Bar in strong onshore winds, it is normally possible to enter the river in a rising gale from the SW. Trevose Head provides the first shelter from this direction and then Stepper Point acts as a breakwater for the bar.

Padstow harbour is the only feasible port of refuge on the N Cornish coast and you should hole up there in good time if the weather looks like turning nasty. The inner dock makes the best berth for visitors, with its sturdy stone quays for lying alongside. The town is amiable and rather salty, and was once the centre of a thriving trade with Ireland and Europe. It is salutary for us yachtsmen to remember that quite large and none too weatherly sailing coasters used to negotiate the Camel estuary regularly, with no recourse to a powerful diesel!

Looking out towards Padstow harbour entrance, with the Town Spit visible just beyond. On your way in, you leave the spit to port and the north breakwater close to starboard.

Above Padstow the river is navigable for 4 miles up to the market town of Wadebridge. The channel is always shifting, but the HM will supply up-to-date information. Wadebridge has a sailing club and a boatyard, but there is nowhere very convenient to dry out. It is therefore best to go up and back on one tide. Along the S side of the river there is a pleasant footpath up to Wadebridge.

Approach and entry

Coming from the NE, pass outside Newland Rock (37m high), which lies just over $\frac{1}{2}$ mile NW of Pentire Point. Then turn into Padstow Bay and head SSE towards Stepper Point, which has a conspicuous white daymark on its N side. Padstow Bay is clear of dangers.

Coming from the SW, having rounded Trevose Head and its off-lying rocks known as the Quies, make for Stepper Point by passing inside Gulland Rock (28m high), but outside Gurley Rock (with 2m depth over it) and Chimney Rock (with 2.3m over it).

Strangers should only enter the Camel estuary within 2–3 hr of HW. From a position $\frac{1}{4}$ mile NE of Stepper Point, head SE towards Trebetherick Point and leave it about 300m to port. Now steer S and follow the buoyed channel up to Padstow harbour. Keep close to the N breakwater so as to leave the Town Spit, just off the entrance, to port. In heavy weather from the W, enter the Camel near HW and round Stepper Point close to, hugging the W side of the river until you are abreast Trebetherick Point. Then cut straight across to the buoyed channel and proceed as above.

Padstow's attractive inner harbour provides the best and most accessible shelter on the North Cornish Coast.

Entry at night

This is quite feasible for strangers so long as there is not too much sea running in the outer estuary and provided the visibility is not less than about 3 miles. The two outer lights are Trevose Head (FlR, 5s, 25M) and Stepper Point (LFl, 10s, 4M), and these should be used to establish your position as you approach Padstow Bay. It is important to avoid Newland Rock and Gulland Rock, which are unlit.

The channel to Padstow is lit as follows: the outer 'Bar' buoy (FlG, 5s); Greenaway buoy (Fl2R, 10s); Channel buoy (FlR, 5s); St Saviour's Point lighthouse (LFlG, 10s); N breakwater head (2 FG, vert); S breakwater head (2 FR, vert).

Berths and anchorages

Padstow Harbour Go alongside the quay on the S side of the inner dock and ask the HM where you should berth. Fresh water is available at the quay, diesel and petrol can be obtained by can from the local garage, and the shops are nearby. There is a chandler in the town, a rarity in these parts.

Anchorage in the Pool The area known as 'The Pool' is just downstream from the harbour entrance, opposite St Saviour's Point. It is really the S part of the buoyed entrance channel and has about 2m of water at LAT. Yachts of moderate draft can anchor in the Pool and stay afloat; two anchors are preferable to stop you swinging out of the deepest water.

Anchorages outside the estuary

Hawkers Cove If you arrive early on the tide for Doom Bar you can anchor on the W side of the river mouth close SSE of Stepper Point lighthouse. Take careful soundings as you draw S of Stepper Point. There is good shelter here in winds with any S in them.

Port Quin Bay If you are coming from the NE and are early on the tide, there is a good anchorage in W'ly winds close SE of Rumps Point and between 2 and 4 cables due S of The Mouls rock (47m high).

Trevose Head If you are coming from the SW, there is an anchorage on the E side of Trevose Head in Polventon Bay. Fetch up about a cable SE of the lifeboat slip and you will be sheltered in winds from between NW through S to SE. Note that Trevose Head is high (71m) while the land behind it is not. This can make the Head look like an island from a distance, especially from the W.

Newquay

This quaint drying harbour is tucked into the SW corner of Newquay Bay, 8 miles SSW from Trevose Head. Space is very limited, but the HM can usually find room for a visiting yacht. Approach from the NE within 2 hr of HW, but don't attempt to enter in strong onshore winds when there is a heavy surge into Newquay and drying out is difficult. Coming from the W round Towan Head, keep 2 cables offshore until the harbour entrance opens up to avoid Old Dane

Newquay Harbour and approaches

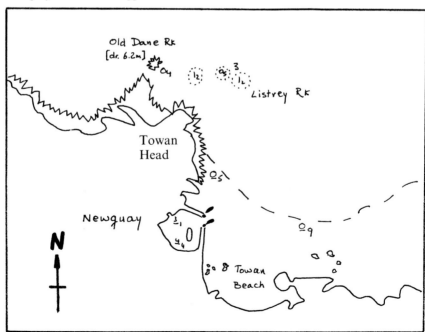

There is always plenty of activity in Newquay's picturesque drying harbour, but space is severely limited during the season. Here you can see the old embankment 'island', which effectively divides the harbour into two.

Rock and Listrey Rock. Entry at night is not advisable, but the breakwater heads are lit (2 FG and 2 FR). In quiet weather there is an anchorage in Newquay Bay under the lee of Towan Head.

Shelter is provided by two stone breakwaters. There are good berths alongside and the bottom is firm sand. Contact the HM as soon as you arrive. An old embankment 'island' divides the harbour and is normally left to starboard going in, but visitors can sometimes dry out on the beach to the W of the embankment; lay a buoyed anchor out astern and take lines ashore.

Newquay is a lively resort, famous for its beaches and surf. The shops are not far from the harbour and there is fresh water at the quay. Fishing boats come and go near HW, or are being worked on when the tide is out, so there is always something going on in this pleasant little haven. There are plans for a marina, which would add a useful deep-water refuge to the North Cornwall coast.

Gannel Creek

A quiet and fascinating backwater not far S of Newquay, entered by way of Crantock Bay. It dries to firm sand and shoal-draft boats can find good shelter by tucking well up towards its head. Choose a period of calm, settled weather when the tides are making towards springs. Come out of Newquay harbour 1 hr before HW, round Towan Head by at least ¼ mile and then steer SW across Fistral Bay towards East Pentire Point. Give off-lying Goose Rock a good berth, particularly on its S side.

Enter Crantock Bay by keeping closer to West than to East Pentire Point, and then follow the line of the S shore round into Gannel Creek. Once into the narrows, keep to mid-channel and go in until you are opposite a short tributary which branches off to starboard. Just above this spur, on the N side of the creek, is a low causeway used by pedestrians to cross the residual stream

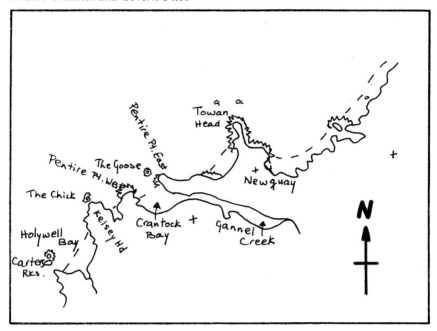

Newquay and Gannel Creek

at LW. There is a good berth just below this causeway, near one or two local moorings: anchor fore-and-aft and take the ground close to the N shore. There are no facilities here and the nearest shops are a fair climb back over towards Newquay.

Do not attempt to enter or leave the Gannel in onshore winds, at night, or more than 1½ hr either side of HW. If conditions deteriorate while you are there, edge up the creek if necessary to avoid any swell which the flood might bring in. Once the ebb has started, though, the effect of the sea is soon shut off.

Hayle

Although now rather run down, Hayle was once a busy little port with coasters regularly bringing in metal ore and shipping out machinery. These were the materials and products of foundry and engineering businesses which used to flourish in the town. Since its demise the harbour has been closed to commercial shipping and is gradually silting up. This is a pity, because Hayle offers excellent shelter once you have negotiated the broad drying flats which form the outer bar and then found your way up to the town quays, which dry to soft mud and sand.

Anyone wishing to call at Hayle is advised to make St Ives first and to ask the Harbour Master there about the present state of the Hayle channel. Adventurous types with shallow draft craft can feel their way in about 1½ hr before HW, during daylight and provided that conditions are calm in St Ives Bay.

Hayle entrance lies right in the S of St Ives Bay and can be identified by two

The attractive and secluded upper reaches of Gannel Creek, a little way south of Newquay. The best berth is on the north side of the creek, just below the pedestrian causeway bridge. You dry out on firm sand and there is good shelter in most conditions.

Hayle Harbour

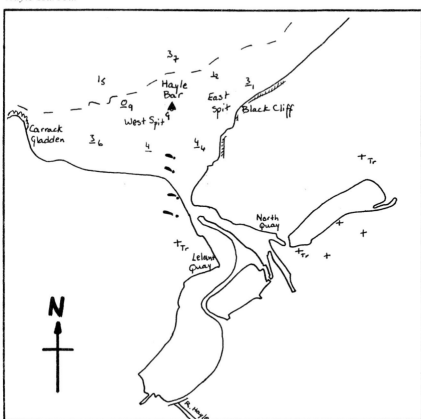

The well sheltered but rather neglected town quay at Hayle. It is a great pity that the port is now closed to commercial traffic and the entrance channel is no longer being dredged.

chimneys on the E arm, and a church spire and two RW pole beacons on the W arm. Approach from due N, steering for the church spire initially. Leave two green conical buoys to starboard and bring the two pole beacons into transit bearing 187°Mag. As you near the entrance leave five perches on a half-tide training bank to starboard. Once inside, keep to the E side of a long embankment and continue upstream until you can go alongside one of the quays on your port hand. The town is nearby.

St Ives

Summary A picturesque fishing harbour, protected from seaward by St Ives Head and by the long stone breakwater which extends S from it. The harbour dries to firm sand and entry is possible above half-tide. Swell can be a nuisance in fresh onshore winds, even from NW, sometimes making it difficult for yachts to take the ground safely. Entry is fairly straightforward from the NE, but avoid the old ruined breakwater which juts out to the E. Strangers can approach at night with care.

Tides HW St Ives at HW Dover −06hr 05min, or HW Milford Haven −01hr 00min. Heights above chart datum: 6.6m MHWS, 0.8m MLWS, 4.9m MHWN, 2.4m MLWN.

Port Control HM Eric Ward, tel Penzance (0736) 790518. Call 'St Ives Harbour' on VHF Ch 16, working Ch 12 or 14.

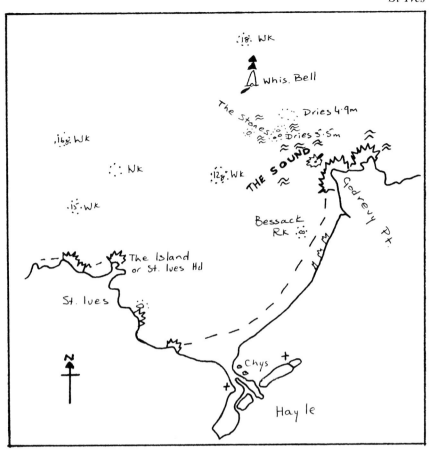

Approaches to Hayle and St Ives

Tidal streams and currents

Streams in St Ives Bay and close off St Ives Head are weak, but become stronger further W along the coast off Pendeen Point. For passage-making round Land's End it is important to take into account that, 2 miles off Pendeen, the NE-going stream starts $4\frac{1}{2}$ hr before local HW and the SW-going stream 2 hr after local HW. Rates can reach $2\frac{1}{2}$ knots at springs.

Description

St Ives lies almost at the Atlantic end of the North Cornwall coast and its attractive drying harbour was once important to the pilchard fishery. The town has steep, winding cobbled streets and is invaded by tourists during the season. St Ives can be a useful haven from a yachtsmen's point of view, offering good shelter in SW gales. However, fresh onshore winds can send a heavy swell into St Ives Bay which can make things tricky for taking the ground.

Outer approaches

Coming from the NE, the main hazard when coming down-Channel from say Padstow is provided by The Stones, a nasty patch of rocks drying up to $5\frac{1}{2}$m and lying between $\frac{3}{4}$ and $1\frac{1}{2}$ miles NW of Godrevy Point. This headland forms the E arm of St Ives Bay and lies $3\frac{1}{2}$ miles ENE of St Ives harbour. Close off Godrevy Point is Godrevy Island and its lighthouse (FlWR, 10s, 12M, 9M), with the red sector shining NW over The Stones.

Between The Stones and Godrevy Island there is a fair-weather passage $\frac{1}{2}$ mile wide, known as The Sound. This is best negotiated by keeping close to Godrevy Island. However, in fresh winds with a weather-going tide the whole area off Godrevy Point is affected by overfalls and it is then advisable to pass seaward of The Stones N-cardinal buoy (QFl, bell, whistle).

Having rounded The Stones buoy or passed through The Sound, make for St Ives Head, sometimes known as 'The Island', conspicuous on the far side of St Ives Bay. If coming via The Stones buoy, steer W for $\frac{1}{2}$ mile before turning inshore, to be sure of avoiding Hevah Rock (dries 0.9m), which lies just over $\frac{1}{2}$ mile S by W of the buoy. If you have come through The Sound and are tacking inshore towards St Ives, watch out for two drying dangers round the shore of St Ives Bay: Bessack Rock, a mile S by W of Godrevy Island, and the Carracks, $\frac{1}{2}$ mile SE of the entrance to St Ives harbour.

Coming from the SW, round St Ives Head by at least 2 cables to avoid Hoe and Merran Rocks, and then steer southwards to leave a green conical buoy (unlit) well to starboard. This buoy marks the end of the old ruined breakwater. All dangers in this approach from N are avoided by keeping Knill's Monument, 166m high and prominent $\frac{3}{4}$ mile inland, just open to the E of the conspicuous Tregenna Castle Hotel.

St Ives

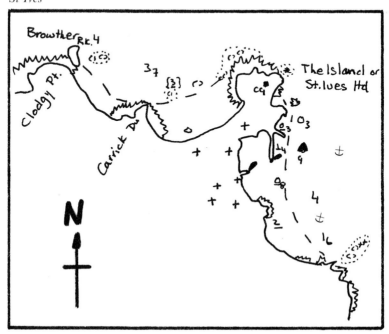

St Ives harbour, looking south towards the main breakwater head. St Ives offers reasonable shelter in strong south-westerlies, but is subject to swell in onshore winds. Visitors can take the ground on firm sand in the middle of the harbour.

Entry

The final entry to the harbour is made from the E, once you are well S of the green conical buoy. Head for the main breakwater head and round it close-to, going alongside the inner wall to check with the HM about a berth.

Entry at night

Godrevy Island is the key light in the outer approaches. Coming from up-Channel is fairly straightforward in good visibility, because you should pick up the St Ives pierhead lights as soon as you enter St Ives Bay: E pier (2FG vert, 5M) and W pier (2FR vert, 3M).

Coming from the SW, use Pendeen light (F14, 15s, 27M) and then Godrevy light (FlWR, 10s, 12M, 9M) to keep a safe distance offshore. Continue E in the white sector of Godrevy until you can see the St Ives breakwater lights opening up behind St Ives Head, and then turn S into St Ives Bay. When making the final approach to the harbour be sure to pass well outside the unlit green conical buoy.

Berths and anchorages

St Ives harbour Visiting yachts usually moor fore-and-aft in the middle of the harbour, well clear of the lifeboat launching fairway.

Outside the harbour If you are waiting for sufficient rise of tide to enter St Ives, there are temporary anchorages outside, either about 2 cables E of the green conical buoy or in the bay $\frac{1}{4}$ mile SSE of the harbour entrance.

Carbis Bay There is a fine weather anchorage in Carbis Bay, about a mile SSE of St Ives harbour entrance. Be sure to avoid the Carracks, a drying ledge extending nearly 2 cables offshore between St Ives and Carbis Bay.

Index

Page numbers in block type denote the main sections in the book for each harbour. Page numbers in italics refer to sketch charts.